# MOUN

# BIKE GUIDE

# Dorset

## by Colin Dennis

The Ernest Press
www.ernest-press.co.uk

Published by the Ernest Press 2007
© copyright Colin Dennis

ISBN: 978 0 948153 87 7

British Library Cataloguing-in-Publication Data has been registered
with the British Library at Wetherby and is available on request.

Typeset by Phil Hodgkiss Design & Print
Printed by Elkar, Bilbao Spain.

**Disclaimer**

While every effort has been made to achieve accuracy in the
production of material for use in this guidebook, the author, the
publishers and copyright owners can take no responsibility for
trespass, irresponsible riding, any loss or damage to personal property
suffered as a result of the route descriptions or advice offered in this
book.

The inclusion of a route in this guide does not guarantee that
the path/track will remain a right of way. If conflict with a landowner
occurs, please be polite and leave by the shortest available route,
then check the situation with the relevant local authority.

It is worthwhile to emphasise that riders should give way to
both pedestrians and horse riders and should make every effort to
warn others of their presence. If you are not familiar with the
Countryside Code, please visit the wonderfully Aardman animated
Countryside Access website:

www.countrysideaccess.gov.uk [England]

Be safe, plan ahead and follow any signs
Leave gates and property as you find them
Protect plants and animals and take your litter home
Keep dogs under close control
Consider other people

## Mountain biking in Dorset

Dorset is steeped in history; from over 500 ancient hill forts to the Tolpuddle Martyrs and the dark harsh world of Thomas Hardy. There is also inspiration to be found in T.E. Lawrence's stirring leadership and Admiral Hardy's ambiguous friendship with Lord Nelson.

Dorset has lent much to the modern world both at domestic and global levels, but above all (as far as this book is concerned anyway) top class mountain bike trails!

A contributing factor that led me to producing this guide book is the place names to be found in this colourful county. Something compels me to visit places with quirky names; what's it like? Who lives there? Where did the name come from? And of course; what are the trails like? Just pull out an Ordnance Survey map covering any part of Dorset and you won't need to look too hard; Scratchy Bottom, Hell Lane, Knight's in the Bottom and Piddle are a few favourites and rarely am I disappointed!

If you've read Bill Bryson's travel book 'Notes from a Small Island' then, like me you were probably in stitches while reading the conversations covering route directions and place names while in a pub! Well, if that's not Dorset, it's pretty close to the real thing and that's from personal experience too. While researching this book I met some very interesting characters who were out walking or cycling and they have contributed in many ways to this book and my frame of mind! I can only hope that I am fortunate enough to bump into them again one day.

The county of Dorset itself only stretches approximately Sixty by Forty Miles; of which over fifty percent lays within an Area Of Outstanding Natural Beauty (AONB) and includes a wonderful network of bridleways, drove roads, permissive tracks and other rights of way disproportionate to its size and status; making route selection for the mountain biker in Dorset quite daunting. Until now of course.

*Happy Trails!*

Without the help of my friends this book would have been a very long and bumpy uphill ride; as it was, these very kind people turned the whole process into a 20km stretch of sweeping singletrack.

To James for switching on my computer, Laura and John at Huckleberry's for the sanctuary. Alex at Offcamber for keeping the wheels turning (and the discount!) to all those walkers and riders who thought I was lost and to all those walkers and riders who were lost!

To Lee for the photo's that made me look good on the hill climbs, her words of wisdom, drawings and food, and last but by no means least, her chaos and her joined up thinking!

And finally; a big thank you to my good friend and riding partner Tony without whose help with early photograpy, computer orientation and colourful words of wisdom I would certainly have struggled; enjoy Australia mate!

**This book is for Lottie**

## About the author

Colin Dennis lives in Dorset and has been riding mountain bikes since 1986. His outdoor lifestyle has provided a wealth of cycling experience, ranging from early mountain biking expeditions to Spain, Italy and France, to organising cycle events, mountain bike skills courses and week-end guided rides in the beautiful and dramatic Dorset countryside.

For more information on the guided rides and skills courses, visit the author's web-site: www.freelancemtb.com or e-mail the author at: colin@freelancemtb.com

# Route Navigator

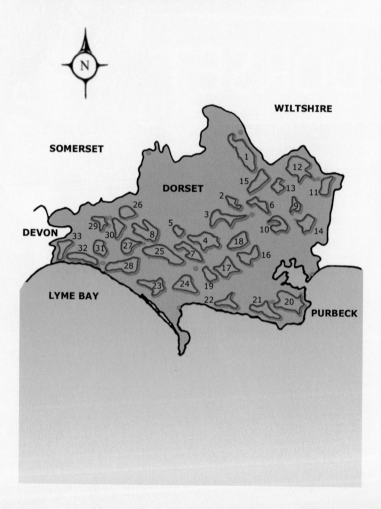

# Key to maps

 North arrow

 Way point

 Primary road

 Main road

 Secondary road

 Minor road

Other road or track

Track or bridleway

 Route

Woodland

 Coastline

## NORTH DORSET

## Grading

I have graded the routes within my own experience as follows:

**Easy** – Fairly flat terrain with little climbing involved but normally includes stretches of non technical singletrack and is covered by good all weather trails.

**Moderate** – Rolling countryside normally with short steep hills but may have long steady climbs and descent and the routes tend to be longer over all.

**Moderate/Hard** – Normally rolling countryside as with the moderate routes but may include prolonged stretches of technical trails and include more challenging climbs.

**Hard** – Add more mileage and longer steeper hills and descents, giving a roller coaster ride around Dorset.

*Looking down onto Swanage.*

## The Mountain bike – your choices

Modern mountain biking is currently enjoying an upsurge in its development. No longer do you have just a mountain bike to ride but which style of bike do you choose and under what label do you ride?

The market is awash with full-suspension and hardtail bikes; cross country, jump, freeride, down hill, enduro, marathon, four cross and single speed mountain bikes are all readily available at your local bike store. Space-age materials such as carbon fibre and Nano technology now play their part in the never-ending pursuit of the perfect mountain bike. Strong, light and reassuringly expensive, carbon fibre is the latest wonder material for manufacturers to wrap around their jigs and produce a bike frame built with the comfort and ride qualities of steel and titanium blended with the lightness of high grade aluminium. Let's simplify the debate and stick with the type of bike that best suited to the routes described in this book.

*CROSS COUNTRY MOUNTAIN BIKES*

The backbone of high-volume sales of all mountain bikes is based around the cross country or XC bike as it is known. Commute to work or ride around the world on it, the XC bike is the universal work horse and to a certain degree will perform any task you ask of it. The majority of XC bikes will have a ridged frame fitted with suspension forks and have at least twenty-one gears. The other style of XC bike is the full suspension version. This is where the main frame supports a small suspension unit (shock) and linkages connected to the rear frame section. Ideally, you will have taken advice from a selection of specialist mountain bike shops and read up on some test rides before purchasing your steed, but as a rough guide ponder on this a moment – generally less is more! The lighter the bike the more expensive it becomes and the lighter the bike, the easier it is to pedal.

Bikes in the low to mid price range hardtail bracket will provide you with pretty much everything that is required; a light-weight aluminium frame, front suspension, hydraulic disc brakes and even a smattering of carbon fibre components. But buy a new full-suspension bike at this price and the component level goes down as the weight level increases! Should you wish to pay more for your bike and begin to reach for the top shelf in the bike shop, you will find that bikes in the mid to high price range are where the fun really starts. The frame may be a specially butted, hydro-formed, factory-built affair and suspension forks with lock-out functions and rebound adjustability become standard. At the upper end of this price bracket the full suspension bikes also become a viable purchase; on these you may find the same frame as on more expensive models but with cheaper components.

Try not to judge a bike by the rear derailleur alone; these are reasonably cheap and easy to upgrade. Look at a bike from this view point – frame first, then the shocks and wheels, this is where you should invest your money. Bikes above the mid to high range invariably become much more expensive for very little weight advantage. In essence, a hardtail frame is a do-it-all bike whereas a full-suspension frame will mainly provide advantage on prolonged rough ground.

**Clothing**

As with the bikes, today's rider is faced with a huge and exciting choice of technical clothing, from base layers and waterproofs to Racy lycra tops with matching shorts or baggy laid-back freeride wear. Even the fashion designer Paul Smith has produced a range of bike gear (in stripes of course!). Prices are available for all pocket depths but the essential items such as helmets, shorts, shoes and gloves should not be scrimped on, even upgrading your saddle will mean nothing without a decent pair of shorts to support.

The clothing is as technical as the bikes (Gortex was developed during the space program) and transferring sweat away from your skin to the next layer is the main function of modern base and mid layer tops. Cotton T-shirts are just too cold and clammy! In warmer weather, loose fitting or square-cut cycle tops are becoming increasingly popular with mountain bikers as well as the standard team race top – just right for that classic cyclists suntan look! Baggy shorts are also gaining in popularity, with a loose fit and a selection of pockets, baggies are a practical choice for many cross-country or marathon riders and have a strong life style look to them, plus a somewhat more user friendly styling down at the cafe or pub.

Gloves are a must, not only do they provide comfort and protection but a sweaty palm on rubber is dangerous! For ultimate pedaling power and efficiency a combination of clipless pedals and shoes are the way forward. Once you have mastered the basic entry and exit technique to the pedals you will wonder how you ever managed without them. But practise entry and exiting your pedals in the safety of your own home before venturing out onto the road and ending up on your ear at the traffic lights!

Needless to say, a good-quality helmet should be used at all times when cycling. I'm no fan of rulings on helmets; it's just common sense to wear one. I would also recommend the use of sports or cycling glasses to protect your eyes from wind, flies, mud and the sun. Three in one sports glasses are a popular choice. One set provides you with clear, low light and shaded lenses. It is adviseable to check the UV protection before buying; however good UV protection is no longer cost inhibitive.

## Safe riding and the environment

Like other adventurous activities, mountain biking is potentially dangerous both to yourself and other trail users. How far are you prepared to push your limits without considering the consequences? Is your riding style potentially a hazard to yourself and other trail users, are you riding alone, did you check the weather forecast before setting out on an all-day epic, are you carrying the correct clothing, equipment and energy provisions? Are you carrying the correct map, did you tell anyone where you were going and how long you would be? Even on a blast around your favourite short trail, some of the above will be relevant. You don't have to be in the middle of Dartmoor to have an accident. Always ride within your limitations and select routes which are within your ability. Riding with others of equal ability allows for friendly challenges and will improve you're riding technique; the ridicule of falling off a 2 inch log should be the worst of your fears!

Ride with respect for other trail users, be they on bike, horse or foot. As the new kid on the block you should give way to others. Ride with respect for the environment and avoid trail damage where possible. If necessary get off your bike if continuing to ride will damage the trail further, even if the damage was done by years of erosion by other trail users. Sadly, it just happens that mountain bike tracks are more visible than foot prints! Well dear reader, you've just ridden 20 miles, saved the planet and preserved your own life, ridden sensibly and arrived back home safely in time for tea and biscuits. How good do you feel?

## First Aid

A little knowledge of first-aid may well go a long way toward relieving pain, discomfort or even saving a life. I'm not attempting to teach first-aid here but a few guidelines or basic instructions and a first-aid kit might just help while stranded out on the hills! First and foremost, it's well worth going on a first-aid course, whether as a first aider at work or as a specialist requirement for outdoor instructing; there will be courses to suit all scenarios. These courses are run by groups such as St Johns Ambulance, the Red Cross or even private companies. If that's not possible or you don't have the time, then follow these basic rules.

*GENERAL PRINCIPALS*

If required, remove the patient from further injury; ensure the casualty can breathe and that there is no danger to you. Stop any bleeding and make the casualty comfortable. In case of serious injury seek medical help at once by calling the emergency services: remote areas may require the mountain rescue team service.

*ANIMAL BITES*

Wash the affected area thoroughly, pat dry and apply a clean dressing. Seek medical help.

*BLISTERS*

Do not pop blisters! Cover the blister with a dry dressing only.

## CUTS & GRAZES

Clean with water and apply a clean sterile dressing, do not apply any ointment or cream.

## INSECT STINGS

Remove the sting if visible with sterile tweezers. Do not squeeze or scratch the affected area as this may help spread the poison. Apply a cold compress to relieve pain and swelling. Get medical help if swelling impairs breathing or of other severe allergic reaction.

## MINOR WOUNDS

The casualty should sit or lie down. Elevate and support the injured limb where possible and if no fracture is suspected. If there is bleeding apply direct pressure preferably over a clean dressing. Apply a bandage and pad, maintaining pressure. If blood seeps through apply another dressing on top. Do not apply a tourniquet. Seek medical help if bleeding does not stop.

## SHOCK

Shock is nearly always present in cases of an accident and can kill. The symptoms are: the pulse may feel weak but beating rapidly; the skin will be cold and clammy to touch; skin pallor; and a hunger for air. Make the patient comfortable and insulate from the cold. Reassure the patient to help allay anxiety and relieve pain.

## CPR (Cardiopulmonary resuscitation)

Ensure the casualty has an open air passage by tilting the head back. If the casualty is not breathing, first check for obstructions such as debris and clear the airway. If still not breathing, pinch the casualty's nostrils and seal your lips over the mouth and blow into the lungs until the chest rises. Remove your mouth until the chest deflates. Give the first two inhalations deeply. Continue at a natural rate of breathing and keep a close watch on the patient's condition. Once the patient is breathing, place in the recovery position, except where you suspect there is a fracture of the spine.

## EXPOSURE

Exposure is generally caused by exhaustion and a severe chilling of the body surface, usually in wet and windy conditions.

This may not be easy to spot while riding in a group but

checking for the signs and symptoms should be every member's responsibility:

> *Mental and physical lethargy*
> *Complaints of cold, tiredness and cramp*
> *Lack of understanding of simple instructions*
> *Slurred speech*
> *Irrational or violent behaviour*
> *Abnormality of vision*
> *Collapse and coma*

**Not all of these symptoms may be present or in the order given!**

All cases should be treated immediately as the condition can rapidly become serious. Always wear or carry good-quality protective waterproof clothing. Avoid becoming over tired and stop regularly and check each other for signs and symptoms. Drink and eat energy foods on a regular basis. If a member of the party is becoming tired, cold and wet, the group should seek shelter and ride if possible along a more sheltered route. Stop and seek a sheltered area for all the party. Insulate the patient, especially from the ground and prevent any further heat loss. Place the patient in an emergency insulation bag and if possible another member of the party should get in to provide extra body warmth. Talk and encourage the patient to allay anxiety and mental stress. Do not rub the patient to restore circulation. Do not allow any further exertion and do not give alcohol. Seek expert medical help. Prevention is provided by good equipment, prompt action and good leadership but is everyone's duty to safeguard against exposure!

GETTING HELP

If when riding in a group one member has a serious accident and is unable to carry on and requires medical attention the following procedure should be followed. Treat any injuries and make the patient comfortable, keep him warm and treat for shock. If the group is large enough and there is no signal on your mobile phone, two riders should make for the nearest telephone, taking with them a map and the six-figure grid reference of the patient, plus as much detail of the injured party as possible. They must also give their own location and stay there until help arrives. This procedure minimises the risk of getting lost or further injury.

Only as a last resort should a member of the party go alone to get help and that person should be a strong rider and proficient map reader. It's worth knowing the *international distress signal* for any such occasion: *Six blasts on a whistle (or shouts or flashes of a torch) followed by a pause of a minute and keep repeating until the signal is heard and a reply of three blasts, shouts or flashes is received. Waving an item of clothing will also help attract attention to you.*

**Bike Maintenance**

The best way to maintain your bike is simply to clean and lubricate it regularly. It is also easier to spot potential problems like brake wear if you are casting a watchful eye over your steed while cleaning it. Try and avoid bearings and seals if you are using any kind of power washer and check regularly for any play in the linkages.

After washing off all that mud, the chain will probably be devoid of any oil so start there with synthetic chain oil. No need to saturate the chain, just wipe any excess off with a rag. Next, lube the cables with some GT 85 or such like and wipe off any excess.

Give the bike a visual check over as you wipe it down, including the tyres and the spokes. Next test the brakes and hope that you have avoided contaminating any disc brake pads by covering them with a cloth or plastic bag before washing! Some disc brakes may not bite as well as they should after washing so bed them back in again with gentle application before going hard on your next ride.

Check for loose bolts especially at the stem, bars and the saddle. It's also worth checking for any play in the headset: apply the front brake and rock the bike to and fro feeling for any play or knocking – if there is, loosen the stem bolts around the steerer tube and tweak the bolt in the top cap, retighten the stem bolts and test for any play again. If you are unsure of any of these procedures take your bike to your local bike shop for a check over or service. Servicing intervals are really down to how much use or mileage you are covering but twice a year is recommended if you are a regular user.

Some components such as front suspension and rear shock

units may need to go to one of the specialist service centres for servicing and repair but hydraulic brake servicing and repair should be well within your local bike shop remit. Some useful reading if you intend becoming self sufficient with repairs is the excellent *Zen and the Art of Mountain Bike Maintenance,* more of a bible really and both the photo breakdown and explanations are very well done.

**Tools**

Never leave home without the following items:

> *Pump, Tyre levers X 3, Multi-tool*
> *Spare inner tube*
> *A puncture repair kit*
> *Mobile phone (fully charged!)*

The pump should fit onto most bottle cage bosses and the rest will fit into a suitable saddle bag or Camelbak. It's also worth taking along any specific tools with you such as the plastic bearing adjustment tool for Mavic wheels or an 8mm Allen key for crank bolts. Other useful items might include:

> *Some long Zip ties/A short length of compatible chain*
> *2 inch section of a hybrid tyre & another spare tube*
> *Small bottle of chain lube/Small rag*

As well as servicing your bike, it's well worth taking time to check the serviceability of your pump and spare tubes and lightly oil your toolS. If you are really unfortunate and split your tyre on some flint then the section of hybrid tyre should fit snugly between tube and tyre as an emergency repair. The zip ties are for anything that should fall off!

I recommend that you carry a good-quality chain tool and don't rely on the one that comes with your 100 in 1 multi tool – ever tried to find that separate thin wiry turn key bit in the dark and in the mud? Life's too short as it is!

While on the subject of time; practise changing an inner tube in the comfort of your shed or kitchen, especially if you're new to this game. No need to close your eyes to practise for night riding, just tune into classic FM, put the children to bed and go!

## Body maintenance

As you are the engine for your bike, why not try and have your body performing as best as it can? I'm not advocating an Olympic training programme; most of us live in the real world, but just as with your bike, some basic maintenance will go a long way to enhancing your riding. In my experience; fitness provides the fundamental element of ability for enjoyment of mountain biking.

### BODY FUEL

Why not be kind to your body and feed it the correct kind of fuel? We're talking about a balanced diet of fresh foods and water. Vegetables, salads and fruit, all have high water content and will provide your muscles with plenty of minerals and electrolytes to help your body recover.

Sustain a healthy diet and help reduce those highs and lows of energy depletion while riding. Food is energy, energy produces heat; and warmth will help keep your body working correctly. Eat well and ride well

### WARM UP

Stretching is not warming up and should not be undertaken without first raising your core temperature and increasing blood circulation to the muscles. Stretching cold muscles can lead to torn and damaged muscle tissue. Begin with gentle rotation of your joints (Knuckles, wrists, elbows, shoulders, neck, waist and hips, legs, knees and ankles and toes) to ease movement and help lubricate the joints and reduce wear and tear.

After your rotations, start raising your aerobic activity and get your blood flowing, then jump on your bike and start off gently before going hard!

### WARM DOWN

This is just as important as warming up. A warm down should include at least 5-10 minutes of riding slower to reduce heart rate. To help reduce the build up of lactic fluid, now is the time to do some gentle stretching off the bike. If you are able to get a massage during your training routine, this will help immensely as it aids the increase of blood flow to the muscles, removes toxins and repairs muscle fibres.

**Hydration**

By the time you are thirsty, you may well be 2-3% dehydrated. This is enough to impair both physical and mental performance. Beat the body clock by drinking plenty of water as part of your daily routine and as the temperature goes up so should your water intake; add a squeeze of lime or lemon if you get bored with the taste of water. Squash and other sugary drinks require water from your body before they can be absorbed into your system; so try not to use over concentrated amounts in your drinks bottle. High-energy drinks should be taken as part of your post ride routine to help replace lost energy and not taken before a ride, as is often the misconception. This could have the reverse affect as they take up valuable water in the body and draw blood away from the muscles and increase the likelihood of cramp. Not good at all!

**Useful Contact information**

Dorset Tourism 01305 221001
Lulworth Army Range Office 01929 462721 ext 4819
Dorset World Heritage Site Team 01305 225101
jurassiccoast@dorset-cc.gov.uk
www.jurassiccoast.com
Traveline (public transport) 0870 6082608
Dorset Cyclist's Network www.dcn.org.uk
Dorset Rough Riders www.dorsetroughriders.com

**Start/Finish Points**

Where the routes start and end at an Inn or public house it is with the landlords' kind permission that we can use their parking and goes without saying of course that it's only polite and a wise move to offer some patronage to the establishment before or after a ride (opening hours permitting of course).

Some of the pubs mentioned are already firm favourites with cycle groups and can be a source of useful information regarding the state of the local trails. Car parking can also be tight at some of the pubs so please park considerately or park nearby if necessary.

# 1. Compton Abbas, Ashmore & Melbury Hill

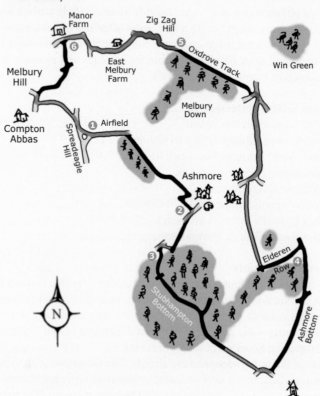

Shaftesbury

Manor Farm

Zig Zag Hill

⑤ Oxdrove Track

Win Green

Melbury Hill

East Melbury Farm

Melbury Down

Compton Abbas

Spreadeagle Hill

❶ Airfield

Ashmore

⑥

②

③

Stubhampton Bottom

Elderen Row ④

Ashmore Bottom

N

Stubhampton

# NORTH DORSET

1. **Compton Abbas, Ashmore & Melbury Hill**
   **Moderate** – 25km (15.5 miles)
   2.5 – 3.5 hours

Start/Finish: Car park at Compton Abbas airfield (ST 891185) 5km south west of Shaftesbury on B3081 Higher Shaftesbury Road.

*Maps*
OS Explorer map 118 Shaftesbury & Cranborne Chase 1:25 000

*Facilities*
The Airfield houses an excellent cafe and restaurant with a real taste for the aces of two world wars. There is also a flying museum and a Falconry centre. Chock's away! Compton Abbas airfield:
01747 811767/www.abbasair.com
Offcamber cycles in Blandford Forum:
01258 458677/www.offcamber.co.uk
Shaftesbury TIC
01747 853514 shaftesburytic@north-dorset.gov.uk

*Terrain*
Steep, rolling countryside with good open tracks and grassy hills. The lower half of Stubhampton Bottom can be a little boggy after prolonged wet weather but is rideable all year round. A short stretch of the final climb can be heavy going for even the fittest riders, so bonus points to be made here for making it non-stop to the top!

*Introduction.*
This route starts and finishes at the top of a hill that, coincidently, happens to be one of the highest in North Dorset. I make no apology though. The facilities, parking and access here are all excellent and the scenery is simply stunning. The route passes through Dorset's highest village, Ashmore, famous for its farmhouse cheeses but bizarrely has

no pub of its own. Close by is the ancient hill top town of Shaftesbury, location of the famous Gold Hill. Forever carved into our hearts with the Hovis advert (you'd have thought the Master Baker would have bought the poor lad a mountain bike though).

I have purposely used just the one Explorer series (1:25 000) map here only because you would otherwise need three Landranger (1:50 000) maps. In winter the airfield closes earlier, so it might be prudent to check the closing times before you set off.

*Links: Ride down the Tarrant road and link up with the Cranborne Chase West route.*

### The route

1. (ST891185) Compton Abbas Airfield. From car park T-L, after 500m T-R onto bridleway following Eastern edge of wood. After 600m take centre gate and continue through field, into the steep valley and S-O up other side. At second gate T-R then L following bridleway signs to the road.

2. (ST909176) road junction. At road T-R. After 250m T-L through gate. Initially, stay next to hedgerow, but after passing around to right of a gate, aim for your next gate in hedgerow ahead of you. Continue through next field to gate and T-R down steep single track. At the bottom, T-L into forest.

3. (ST897168) entrance to forest. Continue on track along valley floor of Stubhampton Bottom for approximately 3.5km to road. 150m further on T-L onto bridleway for Ashmore. Follow bridleway track north through valley for 2km to woodline. Stay in valley floor through wood for 500m to barrier and T-L onto Elderen Row (track).

4. (ST917165) barrier. Follow Elderen Row track through woods for 1km to track junction and T-R onto Halfpenny Lane to road at Ashmore. Go S-O through village for 2km to road junction with B 3081 and T-L. After 350m T-L onto narrow lane, follow to layby on R and T-R through treeline,

joining Ox Drove bridleway for 2km to small car park; carry your bike up to track above car park and 100m further on, T-L onto bridleway before road.

5.  (ST896208) bridleway junction. Continue down track to 50m before next gate and T-R up to road. T-L down Zig Zag hill to road junction and T-L for East Melbury and follow to next road junction. T-R down hill and 250m T-L, up past church and although there is no visible bridleway sign, T-L immediately after dried up pond opposite farm entrance.

6.  (ST881201) dried up pond. Follow the bridleway across two fields and up through the saddle of Melbury Hill, continuing down steep but faint grassy track on the other side to two gates. T-L through both gates to road and T-L. 100m T-L again (unsuitable for vehicles) onto track and climb up to top of Spread Eagle Hill. T-R onto road and take the next L back to Compton Abbas Airfield.

# 2. Hod & Hambledon Hills

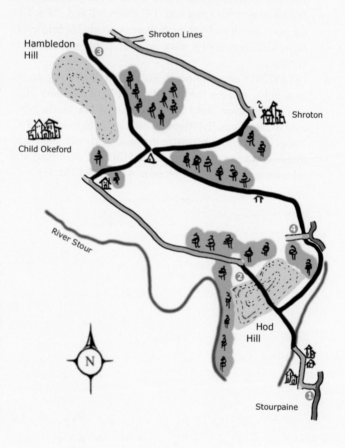

Hambledon Hill

Shroton Lines

Child Okeford

Shroton

River Stour

Hod Hill

N

Stourpaine

# NORTH DORSET

## 2.    Hod and Hambledon Hills
Hard – 14km (8.5 miles)
1.5 - 2 hours

Start/Finish: White Horse Inn, Stourpaine (ST862095) adjacent the A350 Shaftesbury to Blandford Forum road.

*Maps*
OS Explorer Map 118 Shaftesbury & Cranborne Chase 1:25 000
OS Landranger map 194 Dorchester & Weymouth 1:50 000

*Facilities*
Car parking and food at White horse Inn and tea at the post office in Childe Okeford. There's also a shop next to the start for any last minute snacks.
Offcamber in Blandford Forum 01258 458677 www.offcamber.co.uk
Blandford Forum TIC 01258 454770 blandfordtic@north-dorset.gov.uk

*Terrain*
Steep chalk uplands, good all weather trails and grassy hillsides linked by narrow country lanes with top singletrack to boot! This one is for serious climbers and take care coming down the steep grassy hillside beyond the barn.

*Introduction.*
This short but physically challenging ride is virtually on the authors Doorstep and is a classic ride in its own right. Set slightly apart from the rest of the Dorset chalk uplands, both Hod and Hambleton hills are steeped, quite literally in ancient history. Adam Hart-Davis has featured Hod hill in his TV series; 'What the Romans did for us.'. Ridden in either direction, you will find both hills have their own merits and challenges – Hod with its very steep and long climbs at either end and Hambledon with its own grassy single track at the

base of the ramparts, but what they share of course; are the grand views of each other and your next climb!

*Links: Join the Blandford Forest route at Durweston or the Shroton route at Shroton.*

### The route

1.  (ST862095) White Horse Inn. T-L out of car park and T-L again down South Holme lane to X-roads. T-R at X-roads and follow road as it turns to singletrack and Continue alongside river before climbing to gate. Continue up through gap in the ramparts to gate on downward slope. Follow along tree line on left (slippery when wet!), down to wooden gate and into small car park.

2.  (ST853112) car park. T-L onto road towards Child Okeford. After passing road sign for Child Okeford, T-R onto bridleway track at end of first row of houses. Climb to field and continue on faint grassy track to Trig Point. T-L onto track towards Hambledon Hill and follow bridleway down to R along fence line. Continue below ramparts to steep descent; follow around to R and down to gate.

3.  (ST843132) gate. Walk the next 200m (footpath) to track junction and T-R onto bridleway below the telegraph poles; follow to road and T-R for Shroton. In the village, T-R onto bridleway beside the cricket field. Follow track up to L along sidewall to bridleway junction and T-R. climb back to Trig Point. T-L at Trig Point down to gate and follow treeline to left. On reaching large barn go S-O along hedge line and follow around field to R and down to road.

4.  (ST859112) road crossing. Go S-A into opposite field, follow around L to gate, T-L through two gates and follow onto track above/parallel with road. Contour around and climb up to gate alongside ramparts of Hod Hill. At gate T-L onto level grass track and follow to gate. T-L and descend Hod Hill retracing your tracks to the river and back to the start.

*Route 2 Hod & Hambledon Hills:*
*Descending Hod Hill.*

# 3. Blandford Forest

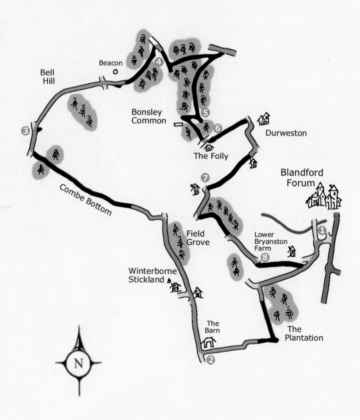

# NORTH DORSET

### 3. Blandford Forest
Hard 37km (23 Miles)
3-4 hours

Start/Finish: Free car park next to the Hall & Woodhouse Brewery (ST886059) in Blandford Forum.

*Maps*
OS Explorer Map 117 Cerne Abbas & Bere Regis 1:25 000
OS Landranger Map 194 Dorchester & Weymouth 1:50 000

*Terrain*
Big hills, long climbs, Good fast rolling trails and steep descents this route has it all, Dorset chalk uplands at their best.

*Facilities*
Offcamber in Blandford Forum 01258 458677 www.offcamber.co.uk
Blandford TIC 01258 454770 blandfordtic@north-dorset.gov.uk
Blandford Forum has all the requirements to stock up for your ride, plus all the usual high street shops.

*Introduction*
The unique Georgian town of Blandford Forum plays host to this epic ride. The town burned down around the same time as the great fire of London and was lovingly rebuilt by Bastards, according to local history. If you want to find out more while you're here, a visit to the small museum in the Market Square is a must.
The riding around the Blandford Forest area can be fast and furious but if North Shore and free riding are up your street then check out www.mtb-freeride.com for a visit to the free ride park at Beacon Hill.

*Link: Join with Hod and Hambledon Hills from Durweston to Stourpaine via bridleway over the River Stour (ST858088). Also, Bulbarrow Hill route from Winterborne Clenston.*

## The route

1.  (ST886059) free car park. Follow road back out to roundabout and T-R, at next round about (Bryanston School) T-L. At staggered double right-hand junction take second R. follow road past Inside Park Caravan & Camping entrance to private road 1km further on for Canada Farm. T-L here following singletrack bridleway to gate. Continue to second gate. 100m further on T-R through hedge, under power lines and follow the bridleway down to the Tithe Barn in Winterborne Clenston.

2.  (ST838031) Tithe Barn. Turn R onto road and continue up valley road through Winterborne Stickland for further 2km to farm access road and T-L. Follow concrete track for 1.5km to Bridleway Y-junction and T-R along Coombe Bottom to steep singletrack climb and follow through two gates to road. T-R onto road for 300m, then T-R onto Wessex Ridgeway (the second & larger track).

3.  (ST795077) track junction. Follow Ridgeway track for 2.5km to road, caution! Go S-A, onto track on to barrier. Carry S-O through wood and follow Ridgeway bridleway along edge of wood for further 500m to bridleway junction in a dip and T-L down steep rocky track. At narrow lane T-R and follow to track, continue up steep climb to track junction.

4.  (ST830096) track junction. Half way up climb T-L, contouring through wood to track junction and T-R. Follow up steady climb, cross open ground and back into woods. Follow same track (do not drop down to Hillcombe Coppice) for further 600m to track junction in cleared area with newly built building.

5. (ST834086) New Building. T-R for 300m to five-way junction and T sharp L onto singletrack, follow down to gate. Go S-O into Glade, follow bridleway up and around Shepherd's Corner Farm to road and T-L. Follow road to Folly Farm and T-R onto Jubilee Way.

6. (ST843083) gate at Folly Farm. Follow the track diagonally through field to gate and continue along valley floor through Sutcombe Wood and singletrack trail to road in Durweston. T-R onto road at T-junction T-R and immediately T-L. 200m further on T-R opposite cemetery onto narrow tarmac path and follow narrow bridleway around edge field to gate and T-R climbing diagonally to gate. The bridleway continues climbing diagonally up L across large field to join track at gate, T-R to Websley Farm and follow track to road-junction.

7. (ST844070) road junction. T-L onto road and follow road around to track junction at Field Grove Woods. T-L, away from the Jubilee Way, up singletrack climb. Follow track around perimeter of field to road and T-L. Continue along road for 1km to house, T-R onto track and follow into farm yard. Go through farm yard to gate on L and T-L into field.

8. (ST859058) farm yard gate. Go diagonally across field to gate and down R to small wooden gate. Follow through woodland to open ground and go S-O towards grassy singletrack to gate. Follow singletrack to Lower Bryanston Farm and T-R to road. At road T-L to road junction, T-L again to roundabout and T-R, retrace road back to car park.

# 4. Bulbarrow Hill and the Winterborne Valley

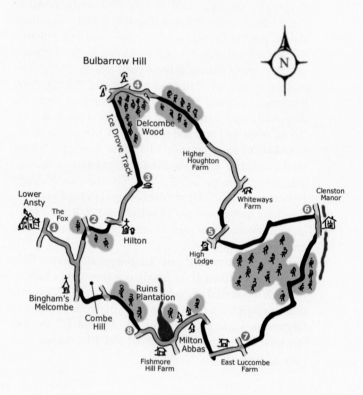

Bulbarrow Hill

Ice Drove Track

Delcombe Wood

4

Higher Houghton Farm

Whiteways Farm

Clenston Manor

6

3

Lower Ansty

The Fox

2

1

Hilton

5

High Lodge

Ruins Plantation

Bingham's Melcombe

Combe Hill

8

Milton Abbas

7

Fishmore Hill Farm

East Luccombe Farm

N

# NORTH DORSET

## 4.     Bulbarrow Hill and the Winterborne Valley
Hard
23km (16 miles) 2-3 hours

Start/Finish: The Fox public house in Lower Ansty (ST765033) midway between Dorchester and Blandford Forum.

OS Explorer Map 117 Cerne Abbas & Bere Regis 1:25 000
OS Landranger Map 194 Dorchester &Weymouth 1:50 000

*Terrain*
Classic chalk uplands linked by; drove roads, singletrack, fire roads and long challenging climbs with excellent steep and fun descents.

*Facilities*
The Fox at Lower Ansty 01258 880328 fox@foxatansty.co.uk
Accommodation, parking, food, and there's a Post office shop opposite.
Offcamber in Blandford Forum 01258 458677 www.offcamber.co.uk
Dorchester Cycles 01305 268787 www.dorchestercycles.co.uk
Blandford Forum TIC 01258 454770 blandfordtic@north-dorset.gov.uk
Dorchester TIC 01305 267992 dorchestertic@west-dorset.gov.uk

*Introduction*
This classic and challenging route encompasses some of the most scenic viewpoints in North Dorset. With good open-going tracks and bridleways, the miles can soon be eaten up. Bulbarrow Hill at 274m is Dorset's second highest point, but in reality is an area covering approximately 1km square, with the masts as the obvious reference point.

*Links: Combine with Dorsetshire Gap and Blandford Forest Routes for an extended days ride.*

### The route

1.   (ST765033)The Fox at Lower Ansty. T-L out of car park and immediately T-L again onto Aller Lane. Follow road for approximately 1.6km, to sharp left-hand bend and T-L onto permissive track. Climb up through Links Plantation to road and T-L.

2.   (ST776029) road junction. After 100m T-R through gate into field, and down steep track through woods. As track flattens out, T-L through narrow gate across field towards Hilton. At gate go S-O onto narrow track, past the church and T-R onto road. *Caution!* After 100m T-L, sign-posted The Knapp and climb for 900 metres to track junction.

3.   (ST788037) track junction. At top of climb T-L along Ice Drove Track. At the end of track T-R onto road. Continue past masts to staggered road junction and keep R at all times, skirt Delcombe Head woods to fork.

4.   (ST788048) Y-junction. T-L and Continue for 300m, T-R through a gap in hedge, into field and after 100m T-L following bridleway between two fences. Follow down through woodland trail to Heath Bottom and Higher Houghton Farm to track X-Roads. T-R onto permissive track and climb singletrack lane to gate. Keep L along faint grassy track to tree line and a small gate. Go between two small trees and follow track to road.

5.   (ST805036) road junction. After 300m T-L onto bridleway down through field and into woods. At main forest track T-L contouring through woods along the Jubilee Trail to Charity Wood. After a short fast descent across a track and up the other side, take track to R leaving the Jubilee Way. Follow track down to edge of wood; T-R out of woods and down sweeping grassy run to the road in the Winterborne Valley.

6.   (ST837034) road junction. T-R onto road for 400m and

T-R opposite Clenston Manor and up into Oatwood, follow track to barrier. At barrier go S-O along singletrack trail past several tracks to edge of wood; follow fence line down to track junction and T-L to X-roads. At X-roads T-R for 500m before branching L onto singletrack trail and climbing steeply up to L. Follow bridleway track around field to road junction opposite Luccombe Farm.

7. (ST819013) road junction. Go S-A at Luccombe Farm for 600m to bridleway junction and T-R. Follow track for 700m to gate in treeline and T-R to road. At road T-L for 300m and T-L again towards Milton Abbas. At the bottom of Milton Abbas follow the road southern end of lake and T-R at road junction. Continue up past farm and on past left-hand bend to track junction.

8. (ST795015) track junction. T-R along track, continue S-O along woodline to road and T-R. Take second bridleway track down across field to treeline and follow down steep hillside to gate and T-L to road. T-R onto road and follow back to Lower Ansty.

# 5.  Mind the Gap!

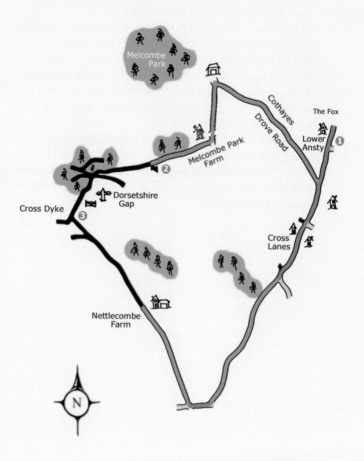

Melcombe Park

The Fox

Cothayes

Drove Road

Lower
Ansty ❶

Melcombe Park
Farm ❷

Dorsetshire
Gap

Cross Dyke ❸

Cross
Lanes

Nettlecombe
Farm

N

# NORTH DORSET

## 5. Mind the Gap!
Easy – 10km (6 miles)
1-1.5 hours

Start/Finish: The Fox Public House at Lower Ansty (ST765032) half way between Blandford Forum and Dorchester.

OS Explorer Map 117 Cerne Abbas & Bere Regis 1:25 000
OS Landranger Map 194 Dorchester & Weymouth 1:50 000.

*Facilities*
Food, Parking, accommodation and liquid refreshment at the Fox at Lower Ansty 01258 880328 fox@foxatansty.co.uk.
There is also a shop and post office across the road.
Offcamber in Blandford Forum 01258 458677 www.offcamber.co.uk
Dorchester Cycles 01305 268787 www.dorchestercycles.co.uk
Blandford Forum TIC 01258 454770 blandfordtic@nort-dorset.gov.uk
Dorchester TIC 01305267992 dorchestertic@west-dorset.gov.uk

*Terrain*
Good all-weather tracks and grassy bridleways bless this compact but eventful route, chalk uplands with a playful note.

*Introduction*
I purposefully chose a short route to explore Dorsetshire Gap, simply because I wanted riders of all abilities to enjoy this magical and remote ancient crossroad. So! Given that you take the route prescribed, this tranquil spot is actually quite accessible, even if it does seem a little daunting on the approach. More proficient riders will also appreciate the tricky singletrack climbing out of the Gap through the woods to the gate above. Don't forget to sign the visitors book while your there too!

*Links: Links up nicely with Bulbarrow from Lower Ansty,*
*seeing as you're parked there!*

## The route.

1.  (ST765032) The Fox car park. From pub car park T-L, follow road for 500m and T-R along Cothayes Drove Road. Continue along Drove Road to its end at large farm building and T-L to Melcombe Park Farm. Ride between farm buildings to two gates, take the R-hand gate and follow track. Don't panic as track ends! Contour around to R of field to small gate at tree line ahead of you.

2.  (ST746032) gate. Head along ridgeline with steep slope to your right and follow grassy trail down into steep gully on L. Go through gate to arrive at Dorsetshire Gap! Head up hill sign-posted Folly and follow re-routed bridleway signs; basically, go up the climb, T-L near the top onto singletrack, drop down onto old track and T-R up to gate.

3.  (ST739031) gate. On reaching next gate at large field, head S-A to large water container perched up high in the middle of field and T-L. Keep hedgerow to your left and follow to metal five-bar gate. Continue S-O down hill, past Nettlecombe Farm for 2km to road junction and T-L. After 100m T-L again and follow undulating track to road junction and T-L. Follow country lane through Melcombe Bingham and Ansty to finish at the pub.

*Route 1 Compton Abbas:*
*Dropping down towards Stubhampton Bottom.*

*Route 3 Blandford Forest:*
*Climbing up from Coomb Bottom. Slippery when wet.*

*Route 4 Bulbarrow Hill:*
*The climb from Hilton.*

*Route 5 Mind the Gap:On the final approach to the Gap.*

*Route 7 Upper Piddle Valley Folly:*
*After every excellent decent, there is an excellent climb.*

*Route 8 Cerne Abbas:*
*Homer vs the Cerne Abbas Giant. A cult classic.*

# 6. Shroton & Smugglers Lane

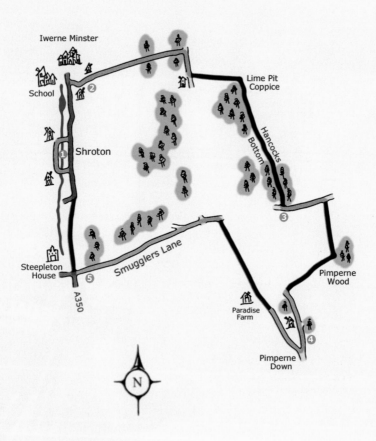

## NORTH DORSET

### 6.    Shroton & Smugglers Lane
Moderate
12miles (19.5km) 1.5 – 2 hours

Start/Finish: The Green (ST860127) Shroton, Six miles south of Shaftesbury, just off the A350.

*Maps*
OS Explorer Map 118 Shaftesbury & Cranborne Chase 1:25 000
OS Landranger Map 194 Dorchester & Weymouth 1:50 000
OS Landranger Map 195 Bournemouth & Purbeck 1:50 000

*Terrain*
Chalk upland and rolling countryside linked by all weather trails and fast singletrack sections. One or two wet patches after prolonged rainfall but perfectly ride worthy all year round.

*Facilities*
Food, and ale is available at the Cricketers Arms. Both Blandford and Shaftesbury are busy towns with all the facilities required to stock up on pre-ride goodies.
Offcamber in Blandford Forum 01258 458677 www.offcamber.co.uk
Shaftesbury TIC 01747 853514   shaftesburytic@nort-dorset.gov.uk
Blandford Forum TIC 01258 454770   blandfordtic@north-dorset.gov.uk

*Introduction*
This route is really a warm up for the link with Hod & Hambledon Hills, should you need one! The long singletrack section on this ride is excellent, not too technical, but enough to keep you on your toes. Also the run down the final few hundred meters of Smugglers Lane can be exciting in low light!

*Links: Warm up on Hod & Hambledon Hills and go for it on Cranborne Chase (West)*

## The route

1.  (ST860127) Cricketers Arms. T-L out of the pub car park, to T- junction and T-R. At main road T-L and continue to road junction opposite Clayesmore School in Iwerne Minster, and T-R. Follow lane up through village for 400m and take bridleway on L between houses to gate.

2.  (ST869146) bridleway junction. Follow the bridleway track for 1.6km to Upper Shaftesbury road and T-R onto road. After 400m T-L for Tarrant Gunville. Continue for 600m, T-R onto bridleway and into woods. Follow bridleway along valley floor for 2.3km to a narrow road. *Caution*!

3.  (ST899122) road junction. T-L up hill. At crest of hill T-R at the well-defined bridleway crossing and follow edge of field to double gate at Pimperne Wood; T-R down hill. Follow track for 1km, on reaching the woodline T-L onto rooted singletrack. At bottom, T-L towards Keeper's Lodge.

4.  (ST903107) track/road junction. Follow road for 450m and T-R onto track sign-posted public route to public path. Follow track in its entirety for 2km to road and T-L. Go S-A road onto Smugglers Lane. After 550m the track splits, stay L; go onto next track for 20m and T-R following the bridleway. Continue down Smugglers Lane.

5.  (ST865109) track junction. At the bottom of Smugglers Lane T-R through small gate and follow track across the well manicured grass behind Stepleton House to corner of main road. Continue along main road for 700m and T-L back to Shroton.

*Route 6 Shroton:*
*View across to Hambledon Hill.*

# 7. Upper Piddle Valley Tour

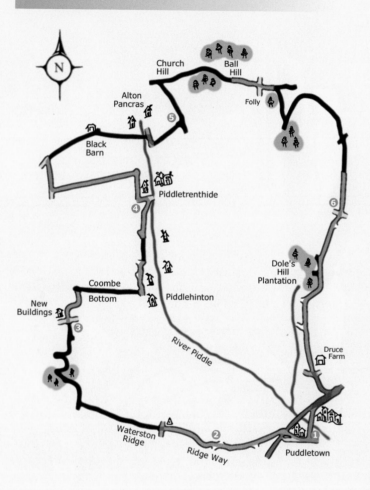

N

Church
Hill

Ball
Hill

Folly

Alton
Pancras

5

Black
Barn

Piddletrenthide

4

6

Coombe
Bottom

New
Buildings

3

Piddlehinton

Dole's
Hill
Plantation

River Piddle

Druce
Farm

Waterston
Ridge

2

Ridge Way

Puddletown

1

# NORTH DORSET

## 7.  Upper Piddle Valley Tour
Hard
36km (22 miles) 3-4 hours

Start/Finish: The Blue Vinney Pub, Puddletown (SY757947) Just off the A35, four miles east of Dorchester.

*Maps*
OS Explorer Map 117 Cerne Abbas & Bere Regis 1:25 000
OS Landranger Map 194 Dorchester & Weymouth 1:50 000

*Terrain*
Classic chalk uplands and rolling hills, linked with all-weather drove roads, grassy plateaus and sweeping single track. All surrounded by incredible views, to be enjoyed in either direction.

*Facilities*
The Blue Vinney Pub 01305 848228 has a large car park, great food and plenty of liquids (ask about the cheese Gromit!) A very mountain bike friendly establishment, the pub is used frequently as a meeting point for local mountain bikers. There is also a shop in the Village should the need arise.
Dorchester Cycles 01305 268787 www.dorchestercycles.co.uk
Dorchester TIC 01305 267992 dorchestertic@west-dorset.gov.uk

*Introduction*
Classic riding over the Dorset chalk uplands with a mixture of all the right ingredients for a memorable day's riding. It may be worth your while stopping off en route in Piddlehinton for a drink and cool your feet in the stream at the Thimble pub!

*Link: Turn the whole Piddle Valley into a figure of eight epic by linking up with the Lower Piddle Valley via the short stretch of road to Athelhampton House. T-R onto the bridleway next to the church (SY771942)*

## *The route.*

1. (SY757947) The Blue Vinney. T-R out of car park, to traffic lights and T-R again. After 200m T-R and immediately T-L onto bridleway at the auction rooms. Follow this track L over the A35 and S-O along bridleway for Charminster. At gate with junction of Gaddy's Lane bridleway, T-L.

2. (SY735944) Gaddy's Lane. Follow bridleway 1.5km to road crossing (trig point 128) and go S-A. Continue down hill, past two barns, to Seagers Barn-Piddlehinton bridleway junction and T-R uphill. At top of the climb follow bridleway R into tree line. On exiting trees T-R, follow around field to broken gate (bridleway sign is missing). T-R and follow perimeter of field to farm track, go S-O past farm to road and go S-A.

3. (SY699966) road crossing. Continue down past farm, sweep R and follow track down L and climb to gate. T-R through two fields and bridleway turns into singletrack as it descends to Piddlehinton. At valley floor T-L following bridleway north, following the River Piddle for approximately 2km, through series of fields and gates to Piddletrenthide to road junction at Kingrove Farm.

4. (SY704998) road junction. T-L for 50m and T-R along track between houses to junction with the BOAT and T-L. Follow the all-weather track uphill to road and T-R. Continue along main road for 1km, T-R opposite road junction for Cerne Abbas. Track descends rapidly to barn, keep R of the barn and follow track to road at Alton Pancras. T-R onto road for 400m, T-L at small post box and join track at the "Millennium Chair". Continue up steep climb to gate. Bridleway splits left and right.

5. (ST709027) bridleway junction. Take L-hand track heading

north towards Wessex Ridgeway and Church Hill. Cross plateau-like feature for 500m and take L-hand gap ahead. Head R and follow Wessex Ridgeway to white gate. Go S-O for 300m to gate, T-L across Ball Hill. Descend singletrack to Folly and go S-A road. Climb track and follow bridleway to R. Top of hill, T-L to track junction at five bar gate. Through gate and T-L. Follow crescent of Lyscombe Hill through two fields; at third gate head across L to tree line and T-R. Follow track past Nettlecombe Farm to road crossing.

6. (ST746004) road crossing. At road go S-A. After 300m leave main track and go S-O. Descend for 2km to bridleway junction at southern edge of Dole's Hill Plantation and T-L. Follow track along valley floor for 3km to road junction at Druce Farm. Go straight across and follow road back to Puddletown, T-R at roundabout and back to the Blue Vinney Pub.

# 8. Cerne Abbas

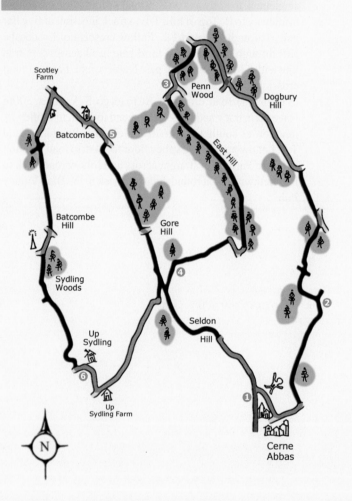

Scotley Farm

Batcombe

⑤

Penn Wood

③

Dogbury Hill

East Hill

Batcombe Hill

Gore Hill

Sydling Woods

④

Up Sydling

Seldon Hill

⑥

②

Up Sydling Farm

①

Cerne Abbas

N

## NORTH DORSET

### 8.  Cerne Abbas
Hard
29km (18 miles) 3-4 hours

Start/Finish: Giants View car park in Cerne Abbas, adjacent to the A352 between Sherborne and Dorchester (ST663015). If the car park is full, try the picnic area around the corner or park sensibly on the high street (three good pubs there too!)

*Maps*
OS Explorer Map 117 Cerne Abbas & Bere Regis 1:25 000
OS Landrenger Map 194 Dorchester & Weymouth 1:50 000

*Terrain*
Rolling chalk uplands with long steep climbs and sweeping descents, interlinked with old byways, drove roads and some classic singletrack.

*Facilities*
Some glorious pubs in the village and a few upmarket shops too.
Dorchester cycles 01305 268787 www.dorchestercycles.co.uk
Dorchester TIC 01305 267992 www.westdorset.com

*Introduction*
This is a toughie! From the gruelling grassy climb out of Cerne Abbas to the near impossible rocky track up through Penn Wood you will find plenty to test even the most experienced of mountain bikers. All this hard work though deserves some fun too! And riders are rewarded with a 2km stretch of excellent singletrack along East Hill and various other downhill delights throughout the ride. Big bonus points to be had for riding the rocky climb through Penn Wood non stop. Oh! And there's a big angry giant to giggle at too!

*The route*

1.  (ST663015) car park. T-L from car park to road junction in village centre and T-L towards Buckland Newton. After 700m T-L onto bridleway marked 'Giants Hill' and climb for 1km to sheep pen and T-L across the field. Pass barn to small wood and T-R along bridleway. Follow track for 1km to singletrack bridleway in small wood and climb through to gate before road

2.  (ST673036) gate. T-L into field, follow fence line to far end and T-L onto old byway. Continue NW along track in its entirety to main road and go S-A *caution!* Continue along lane for 1km and as road descends steeply; T-L onto the rocky bridleway through Penn Wood and follow to road junction. At the road, T-R. After 200m T-L onto grassy singletrack bridleway towards East Hill.

3.  (ST645049) track junction. Follow singletrack trail through wood for 2km before dropping steeply to R and down to track junction at 'Great Pond' and T-R. After 400m T-L uphill towards 'Wether Hill'. Continue for 1200m before bearing L at small copse. Follow track for a further 500m to track junction.

4.  (ST643028) track junction. T-R at track junction, 400m further on T-R, briefly joining the Wessex Ridgeway. 100m on, T-R onto singletrack bridleway marked 'Hillfield Hill', follow to road junction and T- L. After 100m T-R into large field, staying just up from tree line and down to gate, keeping fence line to your left. At next field keep fence to your right and drop down to large chalk gully (the gully spits you out left half way along) to trees and onto road.

5.  (ST623046) road junction. Follow the narrow lane L then R, through Batcombe to junction at Scotley Farm and T-L. Follow BOAT as it sweeps around and up over West Hill. Continue across fields to road junction and go S-O towards masts. Go S-O again to bridleway, past large buildings on left, past second mast (don't drop down into the woods!) to gate and follow track down to Up Sydling.

6.  (ST626015) road junction. T-R, heading SE out of Up Sydling, 500m further on, T-L before ford crossing and climb past 'Up Sydling Farm'. Continue on track for 2km to track junction with Wessex Ridgeway. T-L for 400m to track junction and T-R (yes, we've been here before). Follow this track down over Seldon Hill to narrow road and go S-O. Join the main road north of Cerne Abbas and 300m further on, T-L to car park.

*Please note; if you were looking for the Trig Point at GR ST612038; it's on the other side of the hedge from the track.*

# 9. Tarrant Rushton

# EAST DORSET

## 9.    Tarrant Rushton
Easy
16km (10 miles) 1-2 hours

Start/Finish: True Lovers Knot public house car park (ST 933047) situated at the Crossroads in Tarrant Keyneston, 4 miles south east of Blandford Forum on the B3082.

*Maps*
OS Explorer Map 118 Shaftesbury & Cranborne Chase 1:25 000
OS Landranger map 195 Bournemouth & Purbeck 1:50 000.

*Terrain*
Country lanes, Drove roads and Farm access tracks link this short but eventful route over gentle rolling chalklands. There are no climbs of any significance only a short tarmac hill climb up to the Airfield from Tarrant Rushton.

*Facilities*
True Lovers Knot 01258 452209 www.trueloversknot.co.uk for accommodation, food and camping.
Offcamber in Blandford Forum 01258 458677 www.offcamber.co.uk

*Introduction*
The main feature of this short but interesting ride is undoubtedly the historical WW2 airfield above Tarrant Rushton. With its commanding views of the Dorset countryside, the main runway (now dug up unfortunately) stretches over 1 mile in length running north to south, but it's not hard to imagine old warplanes lining the runways and taking off into those angry skies.
The memorial next to the hanger at (ST 950062) pays tribute to the brave souls who were stationed at this site.

### The route

1. (ST933047) True Lovers Knot. From the pub car park T-L heading N along Tarrant Valley Road. After 900m T-R over the River Tarrant, choose bridge or splash! Follow road through Tarrant Rushton village, T-R uphill to the airfield gate and T-L onto perimeter track. Stay on track for 1.5km to large hanger and T-L. Head for wide access gate and through narrow gap on L. To your R is the airfield memorial

2. (ST950062) airfield memorial. From memorial T-L along road for 600m to Y-Junction and turn R. Carry S-O for 700m and road turns to track here. Continue to bridleway Y-Junction and T-R. Follow bridleway alongside wood for 700m to next Y-Junction and turn L. Follow drove road above the Tarrant valley for 1.5km to SW corner of narrow wood; keep R through the wood to T-Junction.

3. 3. (ST956094) T-junction. T-R and continue along well-graded track 1km to 4-way track junction; turn R uphill just before large silos. At top of climb, follow main track downhill for 3km past Rushton Hill and Dean Farm to road junction. Caution! Cross minor road to Hemsworth and follow bridleway signs to R. Continue along farm track for 700m to the airfield access road and continue along access road to eastern edge of airfield road.

4. (ST956057) T-junction. T-L onto perimeter road to S end of old runway; stay on the road as it swings around heading N. After 300m T-L onto bridleway sign posted Preston Farm. Continue down through Preston Farm to T-Junction with the Tarrant valley road, T-L and follow road for 600m back to the True Lovers Knot car park.

*Route 9 Tarrant Rushton:*
*Crossing the river Tarrant.*

# 10. Badbury Rings & Kingston Lacy

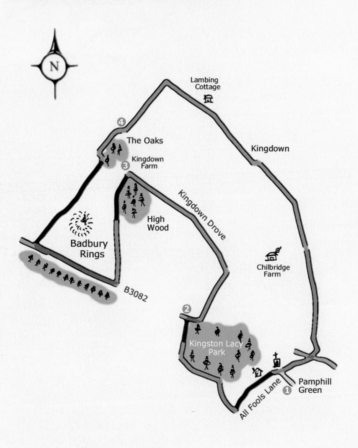

## EAST DORSET

## 10.  Badbury Rings & Kingston Lacy
Easy
16km (10 miles) 1-2 hours

Start/Finish: Pamphill Green car park (ST989007) 2km north west of Wimborne, just off the B3082.

*Maps*
OS Explorer Map 118 Shaftesbury & Cranborne Chase 1:25 000
OS Landranger Map 195 Bournemouth & Purbeck 1:50 000

*Terrain*
Gentle rolling countryside with no hills to climb of any significance but the drove roads, country lanes, single and double track trails of this very picturesque area make this very much an all-weather route.

*Facilities*
Samway's Cycles in Wimborne 01202 882960
Offcamber in Blandford Forum 01258 458677 www.offcamber.co.uk
Wimborne TIC 01202 886116 wimbornetic@eastdorset.gov.uk
The cafe at Pamphill Dairy has a fine reputation and Wimborne can cater for any larger appetites.

*Introduction*
The ancient Hill Fort of Badbury Rings sits commandingly across the main Wimborne to Blandford road from another, if somewhat more recent commanding seat, that of the Kingston Lacy Estate. One is free to visit, the other you pay but both locations should be on everyone's 'to do' list. The trails on this route are a joy to ride, with nothing too difficult other than one short but loose climb right at the end. A couple of sweet singletrack sections spice things up a little for the weekend warriors and the long gentle climbs en route to Badbury rings should warm any cold fingers and toes!

## The route

1.  Start/Finish (ST989007) Pamphill Green car park. At T-Junction opposite church T-L, after 200m T-L onto All Fools Lane (no signpost! it's just before the first cottage). Descend Fools Lane in its entirety to road and T-R. Follow the road for 600m and at sharp bend T-L onto bridleway. Continue on track northward around the perimeter of Kingston Lacy Park. *Caution!* At main road go S-A.

2.  (ST973021) main road crossing. Join grass bridleway and T-R, cross over one track and T-L at the second. Follow well-graded track to next track junction and T-L along King Down Drove Road. Continue up past High Wood and down to bridleway junction.

3.  (ST968036) bridleway junction. T-L and follow trail up and over rise (great rest spot!) down to barrier at main road, T-R on to grass bridleway a few metres before the road. After 1km T-R onto the track leading into car park. Continue through car park to small wood and onto a good stretch of singletrack. At next wood T-L and immediately T-R along-side (the Oaks) wood. At top of wood T-R into wood then sweep L to main track.

4.  (ST969041) track junction. T-L following main track to where it sweeps around sharp R, continue SW towards King Down to 3-way junction and go S-O. At next junction (further 1km) again go S-O along narrow lane. Follow lane for 1.5km to sharp bend, go S-O up steep loose climb to road and T-R. *Caution!* At main road junction go S-O back to Pamphill Green.

# 11. Cranborne & Pistledown

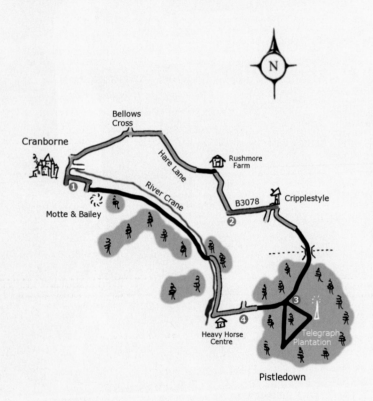

N

Cranborne

Bellows
Cross

Hare Lane

Rushmore
Farm

River Crane

B3078

Cripplestyle

Motte & Bailey

1

2

3

4

Heavy Horse
Centre

Telegraph
Plantation

Pistledown

## EAST DORSET

## 11.  Cranborne & Pistledown
Moderate
13.75km (8.5 miles) 1-2 hours

Start/Finish: The car park of the Fleur De Lys public house (SU056133) down the hill from the Manor Garden Centre in Cranborne.

*Maps*
OS Explorer Map 118 Shaftesbury & Cranborne Chase 1:25 000
OS Outdoor Leisure Map 22 New Forest 1:25 000
OS Landranger Map 195 Bournemouth & Purbeck 1: 50 000

*Terrain*
Rolling countryside and gravel-based plantations linked by country lanes provide excellent all weather tracks with good drainage. That said, the final woodland trail from the Heavy Horse centre can be wet where it crosses the stream, but it's still a favorite all-weather-track.

*Facilities*
Samway's Cycles in Wimborne 01202 882960
Bicycle World, Longham: 01202 590414 www.bicycle-world.com
Wimborne TIC 01202 886116 wimbornetic@eastdorset.gov.uk
There is a good cafe at the Manor Garden Centre just up the road from the start, a village shop and two pubs serving good food.

*Introduction*
This short but none the less challenging route heads away from the Chase itself and covers some interesting ground to the east of the medieval village, after which the Chase was named. After a good warm up on the road, the terrain becomes increasingly challenging as we progress around the route. The 3km woodland trail from the

horse centre back to Cranborne is a real delight, especially the downhill stretch to the river, just keep the momentum up crossing the boggy part!

*Link: This route naturally links in nicely with Cranborne Chase.*

### The route

1. Start/Finish (SU056133) Fleur De Lys car park. T-R out of car park and R at T-junction; continue up through village for 1km to Bellows Cross road junction. T-R towards Crendell. After 1km T-R onto Hare Lane and follow bridleway to Rushmore Farm. Continue past farm buildings to track junction and T-R. Follow track to road junction with B3078.

2. (SU084123) road junction with B3078. T-L for 800m and at phone box T-R for Cripplestyle. Follow road as it turns to track. At end of track continue through field, over disused railway track and across second field to edge of wood and through small bridleway gate. Climb steep loose track and follow singletrack to R. Cross a track to 4-way track junction.

3. (SU093111) 4 way track junction. Turn L onto all-weather forestry track for 500m and T-R just before mast. Continue for further 500m and T-R again; follow for further 500m to original forestry track and T-L back to 4-way junction. Turn L at 4-way junction and 100m further on T-R down a steep gravel hill, past farm to road junction.

4. (SU085110) road junction. Go S-O at road junction to the Heavy Horse Centre main gates. Immediately before main gates T-R onto track. Follow well-defined track down to stream crossing and continue along woodland track for 3km to road junction. At road T-R then L at bottom of hill, back into to Cranborne.

# 12.   Cranborne Chase

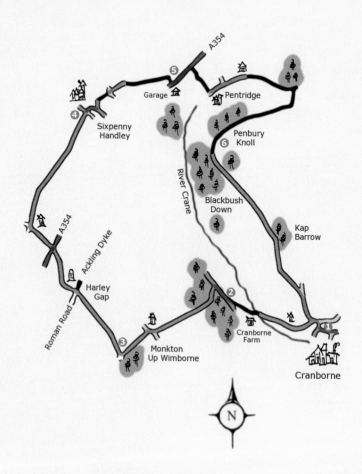

# EAST DORSET

## 12.   Cranborne Chase
Moderate
27.5km (17 miles) 2-3 hours

Start/Finish: Fleur De Lys public house car park (SU056133) in Cranborne village

*Maps*
OS Explorer Map 118 Shaftesbury & Cranborne Chase 1:25 000
OS Landranger Map 195 Bournemouth & Purbeck 1:50 000
OS Landranger Map 184 Salisbury & the Plain 1:50 000

*Terrain*
Classic Rolling chalk uplands with steady climbs and descents. Excellent fast rolling tracks, grassy fields and one small track crossing that I recommend you walk, unless it's very dry.

*Facilities*
Car park, food and Ale at the Fleur De Lys at the start
Samway's Cycles in Wimborne 01202 882960
Offcamber in Blandford Forum 01258 458677 www.offcamber.co.uk
Wimborne TIC 01202 886116 wimbornetic@eastdorset.gov.uk
There is an excellent cafe at the Cranborne Manor Garden Centre.
Two pubs serving good food and drink plus a village shop.

*Introduction*
Cranborne Chase is one of the ancient hunting grounds of kings of old. Here they would spend their time hunting stags and boar and generally have a good thrash around, but woe betide anyone caught poaching. Thankfully, now, a wrong turn gets no more than a hello from a farmer, not losing your hands!

After the initial grassy climb to Squirrel's Corner the trails unfold before you like a carpet. The navigation is straightforward and the going is fast and open, but don't forget to pay your respects to our old friend at Harley Gap. The long descent back to Cranborne from Penbury Knoll is exciting but watch out for a soft hollow in the track that's like quicksand when wet!

*Links: Link up with route 11 Cranborne and Pistledown for a few extra miles.*

***The route***

1.  Start/Finish (SU056133) Fleur De Lys car park Cranborne. T-R out of pub car park and R again to village centre and T-L. Past the Sheaf of Arrows, 50m past the Salisbury Street sign turn L onto bridleway. Follow track to Manor Farm and T-R. Follow the road to Cranborne Farm. Follow the awkward bridleway R then L skirting the farmyard to gate, over the river and T-R through two fields, climbing to the road at Squirrel's Corner.

2.  (SU025153) road/track junction. T-R onto the road and near the end of the wood line T-L through broken gate (no sign post) into the woods and stay on well-defined track down the Monkton Drove track to the road at 'Monkton Up Wimborne'. T-R onto the road and then L uphill following the Jubilee Trail.

3.  (014128) track junction. At the top of the climb T-R. Stay on the Jubilee trail for the next 3km to the A354. *Caution!* Cross the road, past Chapel Down Farm to sharp bend, T-R onto singletrack bridleway and continue on to road junction in Sixpenny Handley

4.  (995172) road junction. At the junction go S-A, down through the village and at the bottom of hill T-L towards Bowerchalke. After 400m T-R along Oakley Lane. At end of track, go around R-hand gate but take L-hand bridleway towards Oakley Down. Follow edge of large field to A354 opposite a garage.

5.  (022177) A 354 road junction. T-L onto A 354 for 800m and T-R for Pentridge. At T-junction in Pentridge T-L and

follow the R-H bridleway uphill to farm. At the third gate follow the R-H bridleway (Jubilee Trail) up to plantation and T-R across field to tree line (carry bike?). Go through narrow gate and head southwest along ridgeline to Penbury Knoll.

6. (039171) Penbury Knoll. From Penbury Knoll follow fence line S towards Blackbush Plantation to gate and T-L along the Jubilee Trail, downhill virtually all the way back to Cranborne. On joining road, head S-O to Cranborne and back to the pub.

*Route 12 Cranboutne Chase:*
*The long, fast decent back to Cranbourne starts here.*

# 13. Gussage All Saints & Ackling Dyke

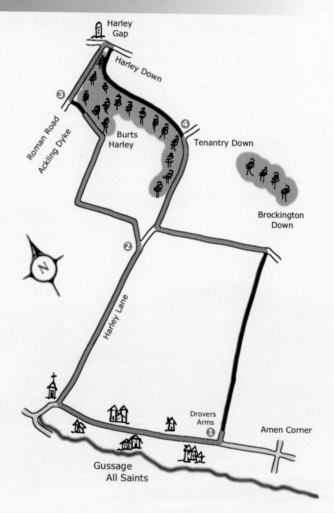

Harley Gap

Harley Down

③

Roman Road
Ackling Dyke

Burts Harley

④

Tenantry Down

Brockington Down

②

N

Harley Lane

Drovers Arms

①

Amen Corner

Gussage All Saints

## EAST DORSET

## 13. Gussage All Saints & Ackling Dyke
Easy
8km (5 miles) 1-1.5 hours

Start/Finish: The Drovers Arms (SU003106) Gussage All Saints, 6km South West of Cranborne

*Maps*
OS Explorer map 118 Shaftesbury & Cranborne chase 1:25 000
OS Landranger Map 195 Bournemouth &Purbeck 1:50 000

*Terrain*
Gentle rolling chalk upland countryside offering up-hard packed stony tracks mixed with soft woodland trails and fast rolling farm access roads.

*Facilities*
The Drovers Arms at the start provides the car parking, food and ale on this route 01258 8400084 Info@theDroversInn.Net
Offcamber in Blandford Forum 01258 458677 www.offcamber.co.uk
Blandford Forum TIC 01258 454770 blandfordtic@north-dorset.gov.uk

*Introduction*
Here's an excellent, short but interesting route for beginners and youngsters alike on which to cut their mountain bike teeth (not literally I hope!) This is a lovely, quiet area away from any major roads or towns and offers a degree of remoteness matched with pleasant and enjoyable riding. This remoteness is added to, by the rather unusual surprise that awaits the observant rider at Harley Gap SU003135. Spooky! An excellent all-weather route for everyone to enjoy before a Sunday lunch! Please note that there are very few bridleway markers on this route, adding to the adventure.

*Links: This ride can be linked with the Cranborne Chase route at Harley Gap, but that might be pushing the limits of a family ride out.*

### The route.

1.  (SU003106) Drovers Arms. Exit pub car park and T-R onto road. Follow through village for 450m, at bend in road T-R, up rocky track and continue for 800m until dropping down to open grassy area to your left.

2.  (SU003116) track junction. Cut across diagonally L and head for prominent track between large hedgerows ahead. Climb steadily for approximately 1km to where track now runs along edge of wood. Follow edge of wood for further 350m and enter large grassy field. Head across L to hedgerow and onto the Roman Road (Ackling Dyke) and T-R.

3.  (ST999128) Roman Road. Follow in the footsteps of the Legions and head NE for 800m to bridleway crossroads at Harley Gap and T-R. After 75m T-R again into the woods. Follow woodland trail for 300m and T-L along-side large open field of Harley Down. Continue along woodline to junction with hard-packed track, and T-R.

4.  (SU010126) Track junction. Follow track for 1km to track junction and T-L up hill. At top of climb, continue for further 350m and T-R at bridleway junction. Follow to singletrack descent and the pub.

*Route 13 Gussage All Saints:*
*Last stretch to the Drovers Arms.*

# 14. Horton Tower & Holt Heath

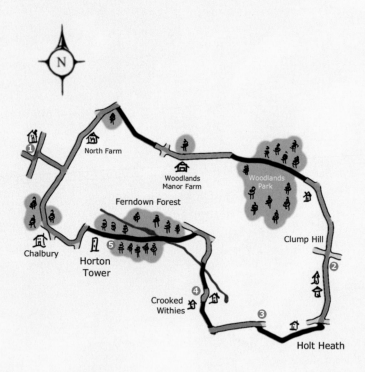

# EAST DORSET

## 14.  Horton Tower & Holt Heath
Moderate – 19km (12 miles)
1-2 hours

Start/Finish: The Horton Inn car park (SU016087) 5 miles north of Wimborne on the B3073.

*Maps*
OS Explorer Map 118 Shaftesbury & Cranborne Chase 1:25 000
OS Outdoor leisure Map 22 the New Forest 1:25 000
OS Landranger Map 195 Bournemouth & Purbeck 1:50 000

*Terrain*
Rolling countryside and open sandy heath land, linked with farm access tracks and minor roads providing an excellent year round all-weather route.

*Facilities*
The Horton Inn providing; accommodation parking and plentiful food and Ales 01258 840252 www.thehortoninn.co.uk
Samway's cycles in Wimborne 01202 882960
Wimborne TIC 01202 886116 wimbornetic@eastdorset.gov.uk

*Introduction*
Built in 1762 by Humphrey Stuart, Horton Tower (the rocket shaped?) was originally used as an observatory for deer. Sadly the tower is now derelict but acts as an excellent navigational aid on this particular route. This route provides plenty of fun and technical riding sections for all abilities, the crossing over the heathland and descending into 'Crooked Withies' can liven things up and the singletrack BOAT near the beginning of the ride is a real joy! Over all, the going is fairly level but the climb out of 'Woodlands Park' beyond the golf course is loose and challenging.

### The route

1.  (SU016087) Horton Inn. From the pub car park, cross the road and head towards Horton. After 900m T-L for North Farm. Continue to road and T-R. Just past the large farm buildings T-R onto B.O.A.T. Follow to road and go S-A for Woodlands Manor Farm. Keep L at large brick gateway. Follow bridleway signs through Woodlands Park, past golf course and continue in same direction to road at Clump Hill.

2.  (SU066063) cross roads. At crossroads go S-A. Continue to road junction at Holt Heath and go S-A to singletrack bridleway. After 100m T-R onto sandy track. 400m further on, head across R towards buildings to pick up bridleway and T-R onto singletrack. Follow to track junction and T-R to road and T-L.

3.  (SU056046) road/track junction. The road climbs gently for 600m to bridleway crossing and T-R following sandy track towards Horton Tower, ignore any track crossings until arriving at t-junction, T-R down loose sandy track towards Crooked Withies. At bottom T-R and then L between two houses.

4.  (SU049053) Crooked Withies. Continue to Holt Lodge Farm, follow track around L of buildings to road, at road junction T-L. After 300m T-L onto bridleway along southern edge of Ferndown Forest. After 500m, follow into forest to track junction and T-L. Continue on hard-pack trail for 700m past several tracks to narrow and wet bridleway track, T-R, follow track to edge of forest.

5.  (SU036066) edge of forest. Continue up past Horton Tower, down to road and T-L. Follow to Y-Junction and T-R for Chalbury Hill. At top of climb, T-R down track, sign-posted 'Horton Inn'. Follow woodline to 2 gates, take R-H gate across field and re-join track. Continue to road junction. T-L back to the Horton Inn.

*Route 14 Horton Tower:*
*Early Russian Vostock Space Rocket, cunningly disguised as Horton Tower.*

# 15. Cranborne Chase West

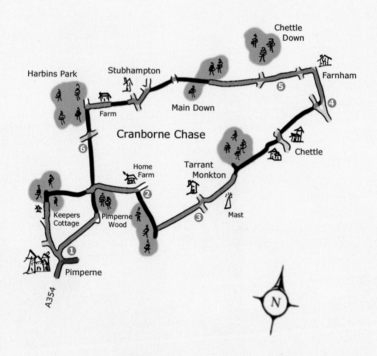

## EAST DORSET

### 15. Cranborne Chase West
Moderate
24km (15 miles) 2-3 hours

Start/Finish: Anvil Inn Pimperne (ST906093) 2km North East of Blandford Forum on the A 354.

*Maps*
OS Explorer Map 118 Shaftesbury & Cranborne Chase 1:25 000
OS Landranger Map 195 Bournemouth & Purbeck 1: 50 000

*The Trails*
Again, the Chase offers up some excellent surfaces for all-year round riding on classic chalk uplands. The tracks themselves are well defined with small sections of singletrack peppered around the route. The only potential muddy patches are at the track junction at the top end of Pimperne Wood and the bottom end of the woodland singletrack towards the finish.

*Facilities*
Offcamber in Blandford 01258 458677 www.offcamber.co.uk
Blandford TIC 01258 454770
The Anvil Inn offers accommodation as well as all-day food and refreshment 01258 453431. There is also a post office/shop in the village and nearby Blandford Forum offers all the usual market town trappings.

*Introduction*
I mixed this route together as a Sunday morning hangover induced no brainer, laced with easy navigation, fast flowing trails and a pub half way around for sustenance. Try it with or without hangover!

*The route*

1. Start/Finish (ST906093) Anvil Inn Pimperne. T-R out of car park, 300m T-R onto Down Road. Follow for 600m to bridleway junction and T-L along fence line towards Pimperne Wood. At bridleway crossroads at northern edge of Pimperne Wood T-R and Follow the Jubilee Way to Home Farm.

2. (ST919123) track junction. 300m past Home Farm T-R onto bridleway track signposted Collingwood Corner. Further 300m go S-O onto singletrack and follow south, along edge of wood. Just before end of wood T-L down the hard-packed track to the Tarrant Valley Road.

3. (ST932119) road junction. Go S-O at road for 50m then T-R towards Eastbury Farmhouse. Continue S-O past masts along byway to Y Junction at gate. T-R, re-joining the Jubilee Way. Continue on byway past Chettle House to road.

4. (ST953135) road junction. T-L at road. 200m T-R at thatched cottages onto Jubilee Way. Follow trail to road, T-R and Immediately T-L onto track, follow to next road and T-L. Follow signs to Farnham and at phone box opposite 'Museum Pub' T-L. Continue for 1.5km to sharp bend and go S-O onto track.

5. (ST946144) track junction. Ignoring any bridleway signs to left and right, follow main track, past New Barn and Main Down for 2.5km to road junction and T-L for Stubhampton. At T junction T-R. After 200m, T-L uphill past water works for 1km to Harbin's Park Farm and to bridleway T-junction beyond, T-L here towards road.

6. (ST906127) road crossing. *Caution!* Go S-A at road; follow edge of field to northern corner of Pimperne Wood and T-R. Continue downhill alongside 2 large fields for 1km to tree line, cut in L down wooded singletrack, at bottom T-L. Continue along track past Keeper's Cottage to road and S-O back to Pimperne. In Pimperne, T-L onto Anvil Road and back to the start.

*Route 15 Cranborne Chase (West): Moo-ments near Chestle.*

*Route 23 Portesham & Hardy Monument:*
*En route to the (Admiral) Hardy Monument.*

*Route 17 Lower Piddle Valley:*
*Childsplay! The river crossing at Throop.*

*Purbeck Riding:*
*Descending towards Swanage*

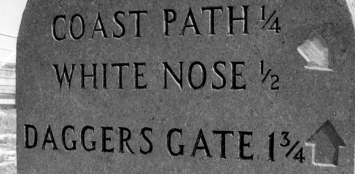

COAST PATH ¼
WHITE NOSE ½
DAGGERS GATE. 1¾

*Route 25 Charminster Down.*
*With the wind is behind you here ... you will fly!*

# 16. Wareham Forest

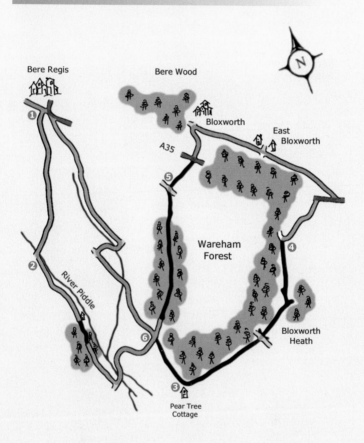

# SOUTH DORSET

## 16. Wareham Forest
Easy – 26km (16 miles)
2-3 hours

Start/Finish – Free car park at the recycling centre beside the church (SY846947) just off the high street in Bere Regis, on the A35 between Poole and Dorchester.

### Maps
OS Outdoor Leisure Map 15 Purbeck & South Dorset 1:25 000
OS Explorer Map 117 Cerne Abbas & Bere Regis 1:25 000
OS Landranger Map 194 Dorchester & Weymouth 1:50 000
OS Landranger Map 195 Bournemouth & Purbeck 1:50 000

### Terrain
Not too many contour lines to negotiate on this ride, but what there are, are covered by well-drained gravel or sandy all-weather tracks.

### Facilities
Pubs and shops cater for your needs in Bere Regis, though the public toilets seem to be going through some kind of regeneration.
Wareham TIC 01929 552740 www.purbeck-dc.gov.uk
Dorchester Cycles 01305 268787 www.dorchestercycles.co.uk

### Introduction
This enjoyable route is really a ride of two halves; one half follows the valley floor of both the River Piddle and Bere Streams, while the other half covers a large chunk of Wareham Forest itself. The wooded section south of the River Piddle is a real joy to ride; novice and expert alike will enjoy the singletrack here, where the small stream crossing deserves mention too! Sand and gravel play a large part here in the forest, and can provide some exciting, loose mo ments!

*Links: T-R at the road/bridleway junction (SY846937) and pick up the track to Black Hill and link up with the Lower Piddle Valley Tour.*

### The route

1. (SY846947) car park. From car park, T-L to T-Junction, T-L again. At T-Junction with Bovington Road T-R and head South for 2.5 km to Chamberlaynes Bridge. Over the River Piddle and after 250m T-L onto bridleway (wide track).

2. (SY846922) track junction. Follow well-graded track for over 1km to small cottage, the bridleway is to the R of the lawn! Continue through wood to a busy vehicle yard before joining narrow lane. T-L onto the lane and follow for 1.5km to bridleway junction. T-R for Pear Tree Cottage.

3. (SY873908) track junction. At Pear Tree Cottage T-L, follow track for 2km to road. T-L and immediately T-R following well-graded track (the middle bridleway). After 700m T-L at bridleway junction and further 200m, leave main track as bridleway continues S-O onto sandy trail for 900m. Re-join gravel track to bridleway junction.

4. (SY895929) track junction. T-R at the bridleway junction (open heathland) and 100m on, T-L. With the heathland on left, continue to T- Junction and T-L. Follow to A35, *Caution!* T-R onto road for 300m and T-L for Bloxworth. In Bloxworth; T-L at the grassy triangle to T- Junction with A35. *Caution!* Go S-A onto bridleway and continue to next road Crossing.

5. (SY873933) road crossing. Go S-A following the track in the same direction through the forest for 1.5km to where, just past the power lines, the bridleway turns into singletrack and leaves the main track to join road.

6. (SY868914) road junction. T-R and follow road for 2km to crossroads. T-R at crossroads and follow road for 600m over Bere Stream to bridleway junction with Spears Lane and T-L. Continue along Spears Lane in its entirety to the A35 and T-L back into Bere Regis.

*Route 16 Wareham Forest:*
*Puddledown Cycleworks Team.*

# 17. Lower Piddle Valley

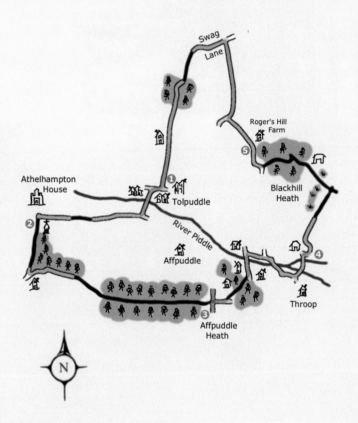

# SOUTH DORSET

## 17.  Lower Piddle Valley
Moderate – 20km (12miles)
1.5-2.5 hours

Start/Finish: The Martyrs Inn, Tolpuddle village (SY794945) Just off the A35 Six miles east of Dorchester. If busy, park carefully near the Green.

*Maps*
OS Explorer Map 117 Cerne Abbas & Bere Regis 1:25 000
OS Landranger Map 194 Dorchester & Weymouth 1:50 000

*Terrain*
For a valley floor, the trails are surprisingly dry, if anything the tracks on the high ground are more prone to holding the water. Sandy, gravely tracks with thin, watery mud on some stretches but nothing that will slow you down. The loose climbs might though!

*Facilities*
The Martyrs Inn 01305 848 249 www.martyrsinn.co.uk
Dorchester Cycles 01305 268787 www.dorchestercycles.co.uk
Tolpuddle Martyrs Museum the birthplace of the Trades Unions
www.tolpuddlemuseum.co.uk

*Introduction*
The willing novice and seasoned campaigner alike can enjoy this excellent route. The ride starts off easy enough but gradually the route introduces some interesting little challenges such as the choice of stream crossings en-route near Throop and the hill climb up to Black Hill Heath. Just dangling your feet in the clear waters of the River Piddle at Briantspuddle can be very satisfying on a hot summer's day. Go on indulge yourself!

*Links: you are spoilt for choice here; either link up with the Upper Piddle Valley Tour at Athelhamton House or from the top of Black Hill join the Wareham Forest or Bere Regis routes. Better still; mix all four. Now there's an epic ride for you!*

**The route**

1. (SY794945) Martyrs Inn. T-R from pub car park and T-L at the green, signposted Southover. After 500m T-R onto bridleway, through two fields to track, go S-O. Follow well-graded track through (what seem like people's picturesque gardens) to large field. Keep close to hedge, to small gate and T-R. Carry on to bridleway junction at church and T-L up singletrack climb.

2. (SY779942) track junction. Follow track up and over the ridge and descend to gate, keep right in field to farm. Go through the farm and T-L onto track to two gates, take R-hand gate and 50m T-L through small gate into woods. Follow singletrack to moorland style field, go strait on and follow the main track as it follows the shallow ridge line for 4.5km to road crossing.

3. (SY804924) road crossing. Go S-O for 500m and T-L onto bridleway for Briantspuddle, stay on this well signposted track to loose and steep descent at Briantspuddle and T-L onto the road. Follow through Briantspuddle village. As the road starts to rise, T-R onto bridleway. Continue for 800m to track junction and T-R for Throop, over river to road junction and T-L. After 50m T-L again along the cycle way. After the second river crossing T-R.

4. (SY832934) bridleway. At last farm building T-L onto bridleway and follow around rear of farm and up to Black Hill Heath. At top of climb, go S-O over first track and T-L at second track junction. Continue along heath land track for 1km to farm; *here the bridleway has been re-routed!* Continue S-O past farm, down steep hill and T sharp L before the bottom; back up steep climb and into Piddle woods, rejoining original trail. After 700m T-R at the

Y-Junction down towards the A35. T-R under the A35 for Roger's Hill Farm.

5.  (SY820950) Roger's Hill Farm. Follow bridleway for 1200m to road and T-R. Continue for 1.3km to bridleway crossing and T-L onto Snag Lane. From the gate at end of Snag Lane, go S-A into open field, follow the well-defined track uphill to L. continue up hill past gate and T-R into small wood. On exiting wood follow the track through two fields to farm buildings and on to metal road. Cross over A35 and continue down steep hill back to the pub.

*Observe offroad areas in Puddletown Forest and the Pink Orange Sub 5!*

# 18. Bere Regis

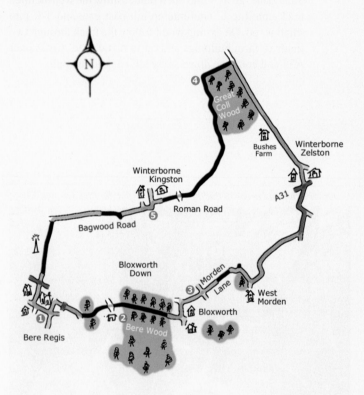

## SOUTH DORSET

### 18. Bere Regis
**Moderate – 23km (14miles)**
**2-3 hours**

Start/Finish: Free car park/recycling centre (SY846947) just south of the High Street in Bere Regis. Bere Regis is situated on the A35 between Dorchester and Poole.

*Maps*
OS Explorer Map 116 Shaftesbury & Cranborne Chase 1:25 000
OS Explorer Map 117 Cerne Abbas & Bere Regis 1:25 000
OS Landranger Map 194 Dorchester & Weymouth 1:50 000
OS Landranger Map 195 Bournemouth & Purbeck 1:50 000

*Terrain*
A mixture of sand and gravel tracks through Bere woods give excellent all-weather riding whereas the chalkier based trails north of Bloxworth tend to hold the water after prolonged rainfall.

*Facilities*
Pubs and shops cater for your needs here. Public toilets are under renovation at the moment.
Dorchester Cycles 01305 268787 www.dorchestercycles.co.uk
Wareham TIC 01929 552740 www.purbeck-dc.gov.uk

*Introduction*
This ride is really an excuse to link up two excellent long stretches of singletrack; the first is in Bere Wood and the second in Great Coll Wood to the north of Winterborne Zelston. The first challenge is the climb up through the woods east of Bere Regis leading to Bere Wood and please note, when descending the steep track from Broomhill, make sure you follow the bridleway at the foot of the hill and not the main track which sweeps left, go S-O!

*Links: Link up with the Lower Piddle Valley route by heading south along the Bovington road to the bridleway at (SY846937) or the Wareham Forest loop by turning right in Bloxworth.*

**The route**

1. Start/Finish (SY846947) free car park. From the car park T-R back to high street. T-R along High Street to North Street and T-L. Follow to barrier and T-R past reclamation yard to A35, *caution!* Go S-A, uphill to farm. 100m past farm T-L up steep bridleway and follow fence line to L and continue across two fields to lane.

2. (SY857949) lane crossing. Go S-A lane and T-L onto bridleway towards Broomhill. At 3-track junction after steep descent, go S-O onto singletrack trail and follow through Bere Wood to Bloxworth. At crossroads in Bloxworth T-L and continue for 600m to bridleway junction with Morden Lane, T-R and follow to road crossing.

3. (SY888953) road crossing. Go S-A road and follow track for 1.2km to northeast corner of small wood in West Morden, T-R onto track and follow to road. T-L onto road and L again for 2km to junction with B3075. Go S-O to Marsh Bridge on the A31. *Caution!* Go S-A to Mapperton and T-L. Follow farm access road for 2.75km to bridleway at tree line and T-L towards Great Coll Wood.

4. (ST882004) corner of Coll Wood. T-L along tree line of Coll Wood to where bridleway turns L into the wood. Follow singletrack trail to track junction at gate, T-R following singletrack to farm access road and go S-A following bridleway along Roman Road to church in Winterborne Kingston. T-L past school to road and T-R to crossroads.

5. (SY862976) crossroads. Go S-A along lane for 100m to bend and T-L onto Bagwood Road (more singletrack than road) bridleway. At track junction go S-O to track junction with the Jubilee Way and T-L towards mast. Continue south along Jubilee Way to A35 *Caution!* Go S-A onto track and back into Bere Regis. T-L onto high street and back to the start.

*Route 18 Bere Regis:*
*All weather tracks and blue skies...perfect.*

# 19. Puddletown Forest & Hardy's Cottage

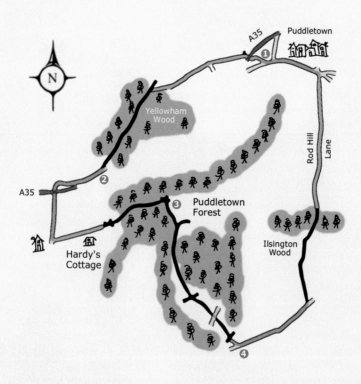

## SOUTH DORSET

## 19. Puddletown Forest & Hardy's Cottage
Easy – 13km (8 miles)
1-2 hours

Start/Finish: The Blue Vinney Pub (SY756947) just off the A35 at Puddletown, 4 miles east of Dorchester.

*Maps*
OS Explorer Map 117 Cerne Abbas & Bere Regis 1:25 000
OS Landranger Map 114 Dorchester & Weymouth 1:50 000

*Terrain*
Excellent forest trails laid on a chalk and sand mix ensuring that the mud flies off when it's wet. Ride in either direction and in all weathers.

*Facilities*
The Blue Vinney pub (01305 848228) serves great food and refreshments plus two roaring fires and ample parking to make it a favourite with local mountain bikers and other outdoor types alike. The village shop can supply chocolate bars and drinks lest ye forget.
Dorchester Cycles 01305 268787 www.dorchestercycles.co.uk
Dorchester TIC 01305 267992 www.westdorset.com

*Introduction*
Puddletown Forest provides some wonderful mountain bike trails by riding on the bridleways alone. There seem to be some unofficial mountain bike areas set aside for jumps etc, but that's beyond the remit of this book. If you should be more inclined to jump or just want to find out more info on riding in Puddletown Forest then check first with the Forestry Enterprise people.

*Links: To join extend this ride link up with the Lower Piddle
Valley Tour by turning R at the end of Rod Hill Lane and join
the bridleway at Athelhampton House.*

### The route

1. (SY756947) the Blue Vinney. T-R onto road, at traffic lights
   T-R. After 300m T-R and immediately T-L alongside the
   auction house onto bridleway. Follow track over the A35
   and head for Charminster. Continue for 1.5km to gate and
   T-L, go 50m and T-L again signposted Yellowham woods.
   Follow the singletrack for 1km to keepers Cottage, go S-O
   at track junction to road.

2. (SY730933) road junction. T-R following the minor road
   up and over the A35; at next T-Junction T-R for Higher
   Bockhampton. After 700m T-L at the red post box towards
   Hardy's Cottage. Continue up past his monument climbing steadily for 400m and past the first 5-way track junction (keep climbing) for another 500m to the second 5-
   way junction.

3. (SY735931) 5-way junction. Drop down sharply to R onto
   singletrack descent. Merge with singletrack from left, T-R
   (still heading down hill) until track flattens and widens at
   major track crossing (Roman road) swing L, down to road
   crossing. Go S-A following well-defined track for 350m to
   a barrier, T-L and continue to road.

4. (SY746916) road junction. T-L towards Ilsington for 1.2km
   and 100m past Ilsington Farm T-L through a gap in the
   hedge. Follow the faint track across field between the av-
   enue of trees and fence line to northern end of field, continue through a gate, skirting field up to Ilsington Woods.
   Climb steadily through woods and carry S-O along the
   double track (Rod Hill Lane) to Puddletown. T-L at road
   junction to traffic lights and T-R back to the start.

*Route 19 Puddletown Forest:*
*Far from the Madding Crowd.*

# 20. Isle of Purbeck: Godlingston Hill and Old Harry Rocks

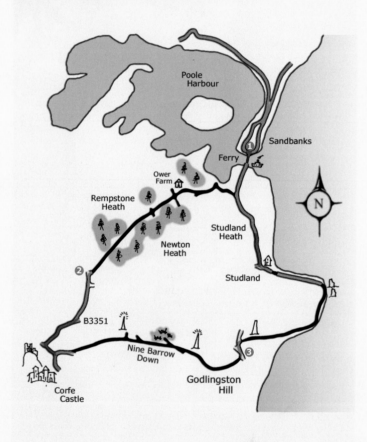

## SOUTH DORSET

## 20. Isle of Purbeck:
## Godlingston Hill & Old Harry Rocks
Moderate – 30km (19miles)
2.5-3.3 hours

Start & Finish: Sandbanks Ferry Terminal (SZ037870) Poole

*Maps*
OS Outdoor Leisure 15 Purbeck & South Dorset 1:25 000
OS Landranger Map 195 Bournemouth & Purbeck 1:50 000

*Terrain*
Large chalk ridges and cliffs preceded by sandy forest trails providing near perfect all year round riding.

*Facilities*
Plenty of shops, cafes and all the standard paraphernalia to be found here in one of the UK'S premier beach resorts of Sandbanks. Windsurf and board schools quickly fill up the parking spaces along the front; so get there early. You will also need a couple of quid for the return ferry journey. Ridebike in Lower Parkstone Poole:
01202 741744 www.ridebike.co.uk
Poole TIC 01202 253253 www.pooletourism.com

*Introduction*
The dramatic setting, the stunning scenery and the all-weather trails combine to create one of the best rides to be found anywhere in the UK. The local riders never tire of riding here (or tire of talking about it) and newcomers return at the first opportunity. Once, as they say, is never enough. As an alternative start/finish point for sea sickness sufferers use the National Trust car park as you enter Corfe Castle from Wareham.

*Links: Link up with the Swyre Head route for even more glorious riding; Heavens Gate is waiting for you!*

### The route

1. (SZ037870) ferry terminal. Exiting ferry and follow ferry road for 3km and T-R at bus stop onto bridleway sign posted Rempstone Forest. Follow main track for 650m to Y-Junction and T-L. At white barrier 400m further on, go S-O to next Y-Junction, stay L again for Rempstone, follow to road and go S-O. After 400m T-R sign posted Ower. At bottom of hill T-L, 100m further on T-R following sandy track across large open field to tree line ahead. Follow track to gate and T-L. At next crossing go S-O for Bushey. Follow track for 2km to barrier and S-O past farm buildings to road.

2. (SY978838) road junction. T-L onto road and follow to minor road junction, go S-O to road junction with B3351 and T-R for Corfe Castle. At junction under viaduct T-L, follow road to bend and T-L onto Sandy Hill Lane. Just past walker's car park T-L through gate and climb up singletrack trail towards Brenscombe Hill. Follow the bridleway markers as you climb steadily for 5km along ridgeline to masts at Nine Barrow Down. Descend to the R on the rocky track to gate, *caution!* Follow S-O down to the road.

3. (SZ018812) road junction. T-L up road for 400m and T-R onto steep track towards the obelisk. Follow the grass track to fence line and take gate to R following bridleway towards trig point above Ballard Point. Continue along coastal track past the Pinnacles to Old Harry (Handfast Point) to where the bridleway turns-L *caution!* T-L! Take singletrack following bridleway signs towards Studland and on to road. T-L at road, at next road junction T-R onto B3351 along Studland Heath back to the ferry.

*Route 20 Purbeck's-Old Harry Rocks:*
*Yes! That's the Isle of Whight in the hazy distance.*

# 21. Isle of Purbeck: Corfe Castle & Swyre Head

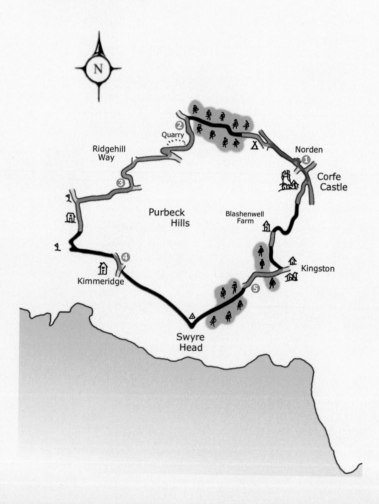

N

Quarry

Ridgehill
Way

Norden

Corfe
Castle

Purbeck
Hills

Blashenwell
Farm

Kingston

Kimmeridge

Swyre
Head

## SOUTH DORSET

## 21. Isle of Purbeck. Corfe Castle & Swyre Head
Moderate – 19.5km (12 miles)
2-2.5 hours

Start/Finish: National Trust car park (SY959825) just before Corfe Castle on the Wareham road

*Maps*
OS Outdoor Leisure 15 Purbeck & South Dorset 1:25 000
OS Landranger Map 194 Dorchester & Weymouth 1:50 000

*Terrain*
Chalk ridges and cliffs provide a varied mix of trails; fast grassy sections, technical rocky climbs and descents sculptured onto all weather surfaces.

*Facilities*
A couple of pubs and touristy National Trust shops provide the basic needs in Corfe Castle, but I prefer the burger van just down from the start for any sustenance (good on you guys!). Ride Cycle Works, Lower Parkstone Poole 01202741744 www.ridecycleworks.co.uk
Wareham TIC 01929 552740 www.purbeck-dc.gov.uk
Classic steam trains along the Swanage Railway between Norden and Swanage and Corfe's most popular 'des-rez' is best viewed from outside the walls (should be nice when its finished!)

*Introduction*
If you like you're scenery dramatic and your trails challenging without busting a gut; then you will love this variation of a classic. I have purposefully missed out the climb up Knowle Hill and inserted a wonderful stretch of woodland singletrack at the beginning (or end). So rocky climbs, descents, exposed cliff tops and sweeping singletrack – this one's got it all. A firm favourite with the locals all

year round. Riding this route should leave you feeling all warm and fluffy inside, it's also a trail that begs to be ridden in either direction.

*Links: Joined up riding with the Old Harry route for another classic all day epic; see you there!*

### The route

1.  (SY959825) car park. From car park T-R onto main road, after 1km T-L and follow Caravan & Camping signs; into campsite to bridleway at top R-hand corner of first field. Follow well-defined singletrack winding its way through the woods for 1.3km to road.

2.  (SY933829) road junction. T-L following road winding its way up hill; at the top T-R along Ridgeway Hill to the bridleway junction at two gates and T-L. Follow down through the gully, swing around sharp L at bottom, then R through gate 200m further on. Continue down to road.

3.  (SY923814) road junction. T-R and follow road for 1.5km passing two road junctions and T-L at flagpole for Steeple Leaze Farm. Go S-O through farmyard (please obey any local signs here!) and up technical rocky climb to large open field, the Bridleway goes diagonally L across field to track and T-L along the ridge for 1km to road junction.

4.  (SY918801) road junction. At road junction T-R then immediately T-L, after 50m T-R up stony track and follow ridgeline for 2km to Heavens Gate. Go S-O to mound just beyond Trig Point at Swyre Head. T-L at the mound, following the signs for Kingston. At end of bridleway track, go across to road.

5.  (SY943793) road junction. T-R; at far edge of woods on entering Kingston, T-L between white arrowhead-shaped railings and follow track down through woods and continue on rocky track to Blashenwell Farm. Go over cattle grid and T-L through farm, follow track as it winds down over Corfe Common and into Corfe Castle. At junction with main road T-L and follow back to car park.

*Route 21 Purbeck's-Swyre Head: The inscription reads 'Jack Bais 1916-1991. He loved the Purbecks'. We all love the Purbecks too.*

# 22. Chaldon Down

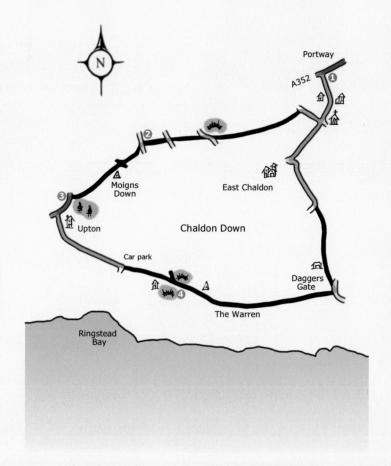

## SOUTH DORSET

### 22. Chaldon Down
Moderate – 22.5km (14 miles)
2-3 hours

Start & Finish: The Red Lion Pub at Portway (SY805853) near Winfrith Newburgh on the A352 Dorchester to Wareham road.

*Maps*
OS Outdoor Leisure 15 Purbeck & South Dorset 1:25 000
OS Landranger Map 194 Dorchester & Weymouth 1:50 000

*Terrain*
Excellent all-weather trails following chalk ridges and cliff tops.

*Facilities*
Large car park food and drink at the Red Lion pub
Dorchester cycles 01305 268787 www.dorchestercycles.co.uk
Dorchester TIC 01305 267992 www.westdorset.co.uk

*Intro*
This is a wonderful ride, full of little surprises and dramatic scenery. Squashed between the more popular areas of the coast line, the riding here is a little quieter and open going.

### *The route*
1. (SY805853) Red Lion pub. From pub car park T-L along Water Lane to church. At bend in road go S-O. After 200m T-R onto bridleway track. Continue for 300m and T-L at junction with bench. Follow well-defined track along ridgeline for approximately 3.5km to third road crossing.
2. (SY766841) road crossing. Cross road following faint track as it climbs gently to large open field; drop down diagonally L to gate in valley floor and take the track ahead

climbing towards Moigns Down. Pass the trig point in adjacent field and bridleway drops down sharply and T-R through new bridleway gate. Follow track down hill to road.

3.  (SY743835) road junction. T-L down hill for 300m to the Ringstead turning and T-L. Follow the narrow lane for 3km through National Trust Car Park to gate. After 300m follow L through bridleway gate; follow track as it climbs steadily around series of fields to Mile Stone.

4.  (SY779811) track junction. Follow S-O in direction of Daggers Gate across open going for 3km to track junction a few metres before the road; T-L and follow track between two large barns. 700m further on at next barn keep R and down the track to a gate. Follow bridleway along valley floor and rises up to gate. Drop down to road near East Chaldon and T-R here following the road back to the start.

# 23. Portesham and Hardy's Monument

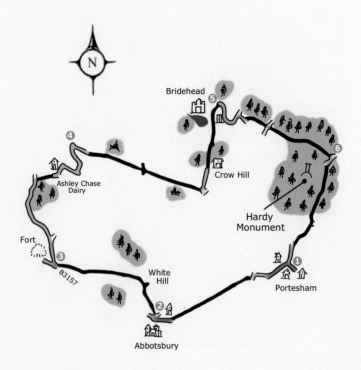

# SOUTH DORSET

## 23.  Portesham & Hardy's Monument
Moderate/Hard – 21km (13 Miles)
2-3 hours

Start/Finish: The Kings Arms Portesham (SY602857). On the B3157 South Coast Road between Bridport and Weymouth.

*Maps*
OS Outdoor Leisure Map 15 Purbeck & South Dorset 1:25 000
OS Landranger Map 194 Dorchester & Weymouth 1:50 000

*Terrain*
Exposed coastal chalk uplands, with good all weather tracks on rolling countryside, topped of with long stretches of woodland singletrack

*Facilities*
Food drink and refreshments at the start and ice creams galore in Abbotsbury
Dorchester cycles 01305 268787 www.dorchestercycles.co.uk
Dorchester TIC 01305267992 www.westdorset.com

*Introduction*
Riders are unintentionally led into a false sense of security here. After the gentle warm-up along the disused railway line from Portesham, the climb out from Abbotsbury is a real test of fitness and determination, so bonus points here for only stopping at the gates.

The coastline is dramatic and the trails are very exposed above Abbotsbury, especially with a strong southwesterly blowing! The fast grassy descent down to the cricket pitch at Bridehead is definitely worth a revisit! And the monument in question is the tower dedicated to Admiral Sir Thomas Masterman Hardy, of Lord Nelson fame. He lived in the village of Portesham from about the age of nine and the tower is built on his favourite ship spotting view point.

*Link: On exiting Black Down Wood, go S-A onto the singletrack bridleway to link up with the Maiden Castle route.*

**The route**

1.  (SY602857) Kings Arms pub. From pub car park T-R and follow Bridport road for 500m. T-R for Manor Dairy, stay on concrete track and follow around L into yard and bridleway is over to the R. Follow old railway track to the main road and T-R into Abbotsbury. In village centre, T-R for Martinstown and 200m further on T-L between cottages onto 'Blind lane' bridleway.

2.  (SY577855) Blind Lane. The narrow track climbs sharply to gate and continue S-O on up through field, ignoring signpost for Lime Kiln. Keep climbing to the top. S-O again until reaching bridleway junction before the next rise. Follow the L-H track to the very top and T-L onto bridleway and follow ridgeline to road.

3.  (SY558863) road junction. T-R and follow for 800m to Y-junction, T-L (S-O) along the unclassified road to 200m past treeline to three gates; T-R though gate across field to Ashley Chase Dairy. Go through farm yard and T-R. 100m on, T-L up hill and follow track around L to bridleway junction and T-R into field.

4.  (SY566885) bridleway junction. Follow along L-hand hedge through field to track and continue through several gates along the high ground for 2.5km to track junction and T-L. 100m before farm T-L towards small wood beside farm and go through two awkward gates. Follow treeline around to R and where ground falls away to right, go S-O along grass track towards Bridehead and down to cricket field gate.

5.  (SY591887) cricket field gate. Go S-O through cricket field to beyond the far pavilion, onto the road and T-R. Climb

up past Littlebredy Farm to road junction and T-R. After 300m T-L onto bridleway (better track access is found 50m further along the road) and follow singletrack trail along woodline to road crossing *Caution!* Go S-A into woods and follow track along in same direction as it undulates through Black Down Woods to road junction.

6.  (SY616878) road junction. T-R up hill for 100m to wood line and T-L onto narrow bridleway; climbing at first then down along sweeping forest trail to fence line. Continue down into valley bottom and climb other side towards small wood. T-R through gate before wood and follow along side wall, through two fields and swing R down to track and to the road. T-L into Portesham and back to the start.

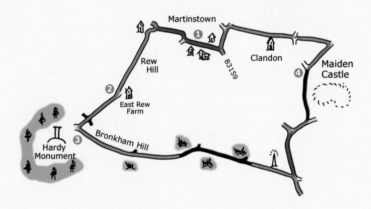

## SOUTH DORSET

### 24. Maiden Castle
**Moderate – 16km (10 miles)**
**1-2 hours**

Start/Finish: The Brewers Arms car park in Martinstown (SY644890)
three miles southwest of Dorchester on the B3159

*Maps*
OS Outdoor Leisure Map 15 Purbeck & South Dorset 1:25 000
OS Landranger Map 194 Dorchester & Weymouth 1:50 000

*Terrain*
Good all-weather tracks and grassy fields linked by a superb long
stretch of singletrack provide the Terra Firma on this route.

*Facilities*
The Brewers Arms at the start provide good food, drink and plenty
of parking, call 01305 88936. There is a village convenience store
for the Sunday papers.
Dorchester Cycles 01305 268787 www.dorchestercycles.co.uk
Dorchester TIC 01305267992 www.westdorset.com

*Introduction*
This picturesque region provides one of the longest and most
enjoyable singletrack trails in the book: the track undulates along
the ridgeline bridleway that follows the (inland) version of the
southwest coastal path. This stretch of the route is extremely popular
with walkers, runners and mountain bikers alike so keep an eye out
along here. It's also worth climbing that extra few metres to the
Monument of Admiral Sir Thomas Masterman Hardy to take in one
of the finest views along the south coast but get there early to beat
the summer haze and the ice cream vans!

*Links: Try it with the Hardy Monument route*

**The route**

1.  (SY664890) Brewers Arms. Turn R out of pub car park following road for 1km along the Winterborne Valley and T-L onto bridleway (road initially) for Southrew Farm. After 300m the bridleway climbs up to the L. Follow the track in its entirety to the road at East Rew Farm.

2.  (SY627883) East Rew Farm. T-R and continue up road towards Hardy's Monument; go past bridleway crossing and up singletrack bridleway opposite Blackdown Woods, signposted Inland Coastal Path Osmington.

3.  (SY616877) coastal path bridleway. T-L and follow bridleway signs along ridgeline towards Bincombe and past Ridge Hill for 5km to road junction and T-L down steep hill. At road junction at the bottom T-R towards Winterborne Monkton. After 400m T-L through narrow gate and climb the grassy bridleway to L-hand edge of Maiden Castle and drop down to car park.

4.  (SY668889) car park. Continue down through car park to bridleway junction and T-L along cycle route 2. Follow the route markers along the track; through farmyard at Clandon and follow farm track to road junction and turn L. At next junction T-R for Martinstown and back to the Brewers Arms.

*Route 24 Maiden Castle:*
*Heading east Along the inland costal path towards Maiden Castle.*

# 25. Charminster Down

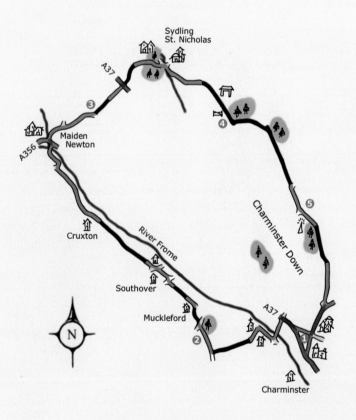

## WEST DORSET

## 25. Charminster Down
Moderate/Hard – 27.5km (17 miles)
2.5-3.5 hours

Start/Finish: (SY676926) in Charminster 2km north of Dorchester.

*Maps*
OS Explorer Map 117 Cerne Abbas & Bere Regis 1:25 000
OS Landranger Map 194 Dorchester & Weymouth 1:50 000

*Terrain*
Excellent farm access tracks and minor roads link up with classic chalk upland singletrack trails for the perfect all-weather route.

*Facilities*
Car parking at the old style Three Compasses Inn Charminster 01305 263618; they sell chocolate bars for your ride too!
Dorchester cycles 01305 268787 www.dorchestercycles.co.uk
Dorchester TIC 01305 267992 www.westdorset.com

*Introduction*
Someone has done their homework and produced an excellent way-marked cycle and walking trail along the picturesque River Frome; providing us with a fun and not too challenging route to Maiden Newton as a warm up. Here, though, the story changes and the climb up past Maiden Newton railway station sets the standard for the return journey.

*Links: Join up with the Hooke Park route from Maiden Newton for a seriously epic ride but allow yourself plenty of time and provisions if you do! If you don't fancy something quite so strenuous, the Portesham and Hardy's monument route offers a suitable alternative.*

*The route*

1.   (SY676926) pub. T-L from pub car park to junction of
     A37and T-R onto cycle path (route 26). At the Muckleford
     sign; *Caution!* Cross over A37 and follow the Frome Valley
     Trail signs over two river crossings to road junction and
     T-R for Bradford Peverell. At Bradford Peverell T-L onto
     Church Lane and follow to bridleway. After 500m turn R
     onto grassy singletrack bridleway and continue up and over
     two fields to steep descent. At the bottom turn R onto Frome
     Valley Trail and follow to road junction.

2.   (SY641932) road crossing. Go S-A into field and follow
     around to top R-H corner, follow trail down to lane and
     Turn L. Now follow well-marked national cycle route 26
     along Frome valley for 6km to road junction in Maiden
     Newton. Staying on route 26; T-L onto main road for 200m
     and T-R for Cattistock. 400m on T-R onto Station Road
     and continue up under bridge and climb the well-graded
     bridleway track to the Bridleway junction at the top. (Don't
     be tempted to follow the Wessex Ridgeway near the top.)

3.   (SY607982) bridleway junction. T-L and follow grass track
     to farm yard, continue on through to the A37. *Caution!* Go
     S-A and follow the bridleway (Wessex Ridgeway) signs
     down through a series of fields to high hedge track and
     follow down to barrier and S-O to crossroads in Sydling St
     Nicolas. At crossroads T-R and after 500m Turn L onto
     bridleway for Huish. Follow track past sheep pens and L
     up steep concrete track. Top of climb; go S-O onto fast
     grassy descent. Keep in valley floor, past large tin barn to
     gate.

4.   (SY650981) gate. 200m past gate T-L onto narrow grass
     track and up steep hillside (no signpost here) to gate.
     Continue up through gate to bridleway junction on ridgeline
     ahead and T-R. Follow ridgeline bridleway south (that's
     the Hardy monument in the far distance) for 1500m to wide
     gate at three-way bridleway junction.

5. (SY652965) bridleway junction. T-L through second gate following track towards large mast and continue S-O along edge of wood to gate. Keep L onto grass singletrack for 500m then join faint track around to R and follow to gate (do not follow trail down to Forston). Head S and then southeast for 2km following bridleway signs for Charminster, join road and go S-O. At crossroads in Charminster T-R. 200m further on, T-R again and back to the pub.

# 26. Melbury Osmond

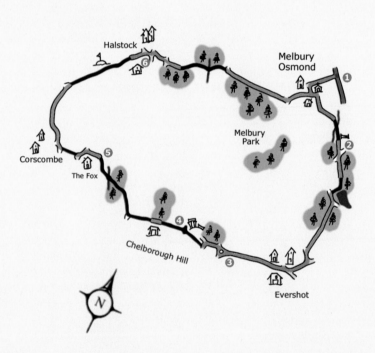

## WEST DORSET

### 26. Melbury Osmond
Moderate/Hard – 22.5km (14miles)
2-3 hours

Start/Finish: The car park of the Rest & Welcome Inn (ST078582) on the A37 at Melbury Osmond between Dorchester and Yeovil.

*Maps*
OS Explorer Map 11 7 Cerne Abbas & Bere Regis 1: 25 000
OS Landranger Map 194 Dorchester & Weymouth 1: 50 000

*Terrain*
Potentially wet in a few areas along the way but nothing to slow you down too much

*Facilities*
Food, drink and parking at the Rest & Welcome Inn
Dorchester Cycles 01305 268787 www.dorchestercycles.co.uk
Dorchester TIC 01305 267992 www.westdorset.com

*Introduction*
This stand alone route is certainly worth the journey, is quite a mini adventure in itself and has all the right ingredients to satisfy the week-end warrior and marathon/epic rider alike. With its long technical descent, interesting woodland sections and a spooky sunken lane, here is a route on which to hone those rusty techniques in an alternative Dorset location.

*The Route*
1.  (ST078582) The Rest and Welcome Inn. T-R out of car park and next L for Melbury Osmond. Follow to village and follow around L through the village. At sharp R-hand bend below the village follow the bridleway sign off to the

L. Follow down through tunnel and over (through?) stream and along the sunken lane to gate.

2. (ST578075) gate. Go S-A to R-hand bridleway gate and follow track to access road, go S-A heading towards the lake. T-R then L following bridleway around lake and T-L uphill towards Evershot. At road junction T-L to main road (the common) and T-R. Continue up through Evershot for 2km to road junction.

3. (ST557044) road junction. T-R towards West Chelborough and S-O at X-roads to sharp bend in road; T-L up small lane towards Hemlock Farm and T-R immediately up narrow gulley. Follow across fields to Chelborough Hill. Keeping the small stone circle on your R, at fence line go strait on through two awkward bridleway gates at bridleway junction and into next field.

4. (ST544046) bridleway junction. With fence line on L, head towards large barn ahead and up to a gate. Follow the track ahead to bridleway junction and T-R downhill through a field to wood. Continue into the wood along singletrack trail to where trail cuts L across the stream and up to a gate, follow tree line downhill to gate and join the narrow access track.

5. (ST532053) access track. T-L onto access track and at next road junction Turn L. T-R just past the Fox Inn and at next junction T-R again. On entering Corscombe T-R onto unclassified road and follow track around past water works and continue up and over Wood Fold Hill. Continue along the length of Common Lane in its entirety; past the golf course and into Halstock.

6. (ST538079) road junction. T-R and T-L onto main road in Halstock. 150m along road T-R along cycle route 26 uphill to Clarkham Cross. Go S-A onto bridleway track and continue onto singletrack trail through wood to gate. T-L into field and down again through small wood. Go over stream and up through boggy track to field. Follow around

to R to join main track at top of field and T-L towards Melbury Osmond. At road junction in village T-L and follow road back through village to the start.

# 27. Hooke Park & Eggardon Hill

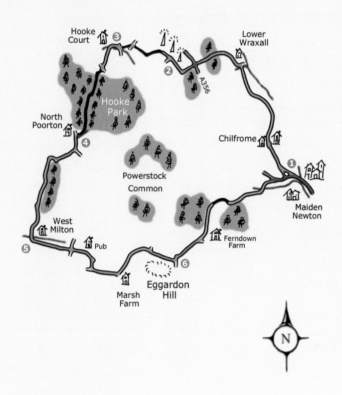

Hooke Court 3

Hooke Park

North Poorton 4

Lower Wraxall

A356

Chilfrome 1

Maiden Newton

2

Powerstock Common

West Milton 5

Pub

Ferndown Farm 6

Marsh Farm

Eggardon Hill

N

## WEST DORSET

## 27. Hooke Park & Eggardon Hill
Hard – 28km (17.5miles)
3-4 hours

Start/Finish: Small car park adjacent the primary school (SY593979) along the Chilfrome road in Maiden Newton. Maiden Newton is on the A356 Dorchester to Crewkerne road.

*Maps*
OS Explorer Map 117 Cerne Abbas & Bere Regis 1:25 000
OS Landranger Map 194 Dorchester & Weymouth 1:50 000

*Terrain*
Rolling chalk uplands linked by steep valleys, forest trails and excellent all-weather technical trails.

*Facilities*
Pubs, shops and all the local facilities that a large village has to offer; plus a railway station which is useful if you can get your bike on a train these days.
Dorchester Cycles 01305 268787 www.dorchestercycles.co.uk
Dorchester TIC 01305 267992 www.westdorset.com

*Introduction*
Maiden Newton has been an excellent start point for much of my riding over the years; as access to all the wonderful trails here is simple and navigation straight forward enough. Head off in any direction and you won't need to look too hard for terrific riding for all abilities.

*Links: If your legs are up for it link up the Charminster route or the Eggardon Hill route from the summit of the ancient fort. The Beaminster East route meets up at North Porton for an alternative link up.*

## The route

1.  (SY593979) car park. T-L and follow road to Chilfrome. Go S-O at cross roads to track and continue along Wraxhall Lane to ford crossing at road junction in Lower Wraxhall. T-L onto road and follow up to road junction with A 356 *Caution!* T-R onto main road then T-L onto narrow lane before masts and follow for 800m to sharp L-hand bend; go S-O to track junction.

2.  (ST549007) track junction. Continue along track down past masts to narrow bridleway gate. Drop into valley floor for 100m and climb to bridleway gate (hidden by tree) at hedge line up to R. Follow through field to join track and down to road. Go S-A onto narrow track and continue past small group of houses to road junction.

3.  (ST005534) road junction. T-R onto road and climb past Hooke Court to road junction. Go S-A to bridleway and T-L onto main track and follow for 400m to track junction and T-R down to small hut. T-L at hut and follow damp singletrack trail down through Hooke Park; across one track to stream crossing and into field. Climb to gate and T-R down to gate at tree line. Follow rocky track along (above) stream to road junction at North Poorton.

4.  (SY520985) North Poorton. T-L onto road to South Poorton and follow road around to R. Continue along road for 1.5km past one bridleway to narrow wood line on L; continue on road for 100m (getting steeper) and T-L through narrow gap onto steep singletrack trail and descend for 1200m to road. T-L through West Milton to road junction.

5.  (SY501963) road junction. T-L towards Powerstock to cross roads; go S-O towards Nettlecombe and the Marquis of Lorne pub. Keep R at pub to road junction and T-L. At

Y-junction T-L towards Marsh Farm and follow track up northwest side of Eggardon Hill to narrow road. T-R along Eggardon Hill to road junction.

6.  (SY546945) road junction. T-L and 250m on T-R towards Maiden Newton. Continue along road for 2km to sharp bend and go S-O to track. At entrance to Ferndown Farm T-L through gate into field and follow hedge line below farm to broken wooden gate. Rejoin track and continue down to Toller Fratrum and to A 356. T-R into Maiden Newton and T-L towards Chilfrome back to the start.

# 28. Eggardon Hill

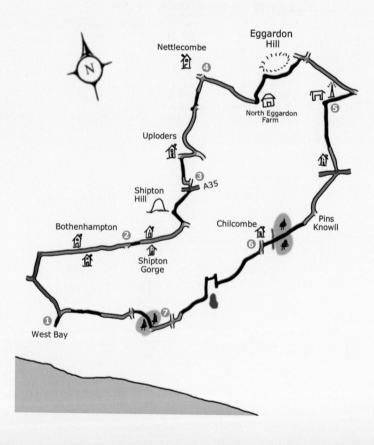

## WEST DORSET

### 28.　Eggardon Hill
Hard – 32.5km (20 Miles)
4-5 hours

Start/Finish: Long stay car park (SY466906) in West Bay Bridport

*Maps*
OS Explorer Map 116 Lyme Regis & Bridport 1:25 000
OS Explorer Map 117 Cerne Abbas & Bere Regis 1:25 000
OS Landranger Map 193
OS Landranger Map194 Dorchester & Weymouth 1:50 000

*Terrain*
Steep chalk uplands and valleys with rolling coastal countryside linked by an excellent mix of all-weather singletrack trails bridleway tracks and country lanes.

*Facilities*
West Bay has an eclectic mix of watering holes and eating houses catering for all tastes. Plenty of B&B establishments grace the road leading into West Bay should you want to stop over.
Revolutions in Bridport 01308 420586
Bridport TIC 01308 424901 www.westdorset.com

*Introduction*
What better place to start one of the toughest and challenging routes in this book than at sea level; just to get the full benefit of the climbing involved of course! On reaching the roof top of Eggardon Hill, the views seem to stretch on forever in every direction (fog permitting!) and the scenery stretching northwards to Beaminster and across to Pilsdon Penn (Dorset's Highest Point) displays the topography of this beautiful region to dramatic effect.

*Links: If you have any energy and time left; link up with the Jurassic Coast route or the slightly less challenging Hell Lane ride and of course; the Hooke Park loop.*

### The route

1.  (SY466906) car park. Join national cycle route 2 at rear of car park and T-L, follow to road junction. T-L and follow to roundabout taking fourth exit (A35). Follow to road junction signposted Bothenhampton and T-R. Continue through village and S-O to track alongside Gentlemen's Club? up to road junction; continue S-O for 1km to track junction and gate

2.  (SY484916) track junction. Go S-O through gate along faint track to narrow bridleway gate and climb singletrack trail to road junction. Go S-O through Shipton Gorge and take the Dorchester road. 100m past Higher Sturhill Farm T-L onto bridleway opposite sharp bend. Follow track to base of Shipton Hill; T-R at bridleway post and follow around to gate. T-R across field towards gap in hedge row and descend to A35.

3.  (SY509928) A35. Caution! Go S-A onto minor road and T-L at post box. Go past houses and T-R onto track and descend to road at Uploaders. T-R to sharp bend and T-L past Matravers Farm to bridleway junction and follow around R. Continue to track junction of disused railway line and go diagonally across field ahead (there seems to be no provision to navigate around the field here; and of course there is no right of way if you turn right and then left at the next track; so don't do it!) to unclassified road and on to crossroads.

4.  (SY517954) crossroads. T-R onto road and keep R at Y-junction for 1.5km to North Eggardon Farm. Follow bridleway to L of farm and climb singletrack up face of Eggardon Hill to gate. Go beyond first rampart and T-R contouring up to hill top. Go though gate at top and T-L through narrow bridleway gate into field and across to road.

T-R to crossroads and go S-A for 1km to track junction and T-R back towards mast and barn.

5. (SY548939) barn & gate. Go through gate and immediately T-L alongside field to bridleway gate. Head S-A open field to pylons beyond, keeping R along thin tree line ahead and follow track down to Stancombe Farm. Climb access road to A35. Caution! Go S-A down narrow lane for 1300 metres to steep sharp left bend and T-R onto track. Stay on level grass track and follow bridleway signs through gate and down to L. At second gate; head across field towards boggy stream and climb S-O up across two fields to road crossing at Chilcombe.

6. (SY527908) road crossing. T-L and immediately T-R onto bridleway. At gate follow down L of field and sweep around R of small knoll to gate. T-R onto track for 300m and T-L at bridleway junction. Follow for 400m to bridleway junction and T-L towards fishing lake. Head R past lake to gate and follow sunken lane through wood to field. Head up field below Bready North Hill, to narrow gate and follow edge of wood into following field. Head S-O to far end of field to gate and continue S-O along track to crossroads.

7. (SY506902) crossroads. Continue S-O along road 700m to small wood and T-R onto bridleway. Climb singletrack through wood; across two fields and at third gate T-L toward houses. Follow track to road and T-L then T-R along lane. Carry S-O along track following along high ground and down singletrack descent to road. Continue S-O down singletrack to main road crossing. Go S-A and T-L onto original cycle path and return to start.

# 29. Beaminster and the West

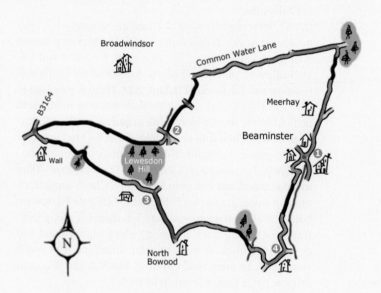

Broadwindsor

Common Water Lane

B3164

Wall

Meerhay

Beaminster

Lewesdon
Hill

North
Bowood

N

Route 27 Hooke Park & Eggardon Hill:
Deep in the forest ... something stirred!

*Route 28 Eggardon Hill.*
*Turn right on steep, sharp bend.*

# 30. Beaminster & the East

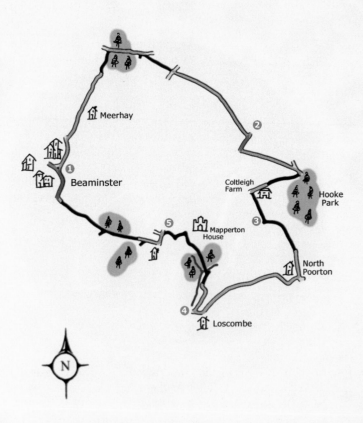

Meerhay

Beaminster

Coltleigh
Farm

Hooke
Park

Mapperton
House

North
Poorton

Loscombe

N

**West Dorset**

## 30.  Beaminster & the East
Moderate/Hard – 20km (12.5miles)
2-3 hours

Start/Finish: Pay & display car park (ST482014) off Fleet St in the
centre of Beaminster, six miles North of Bridport.

*Maps*
OS Explorer Map 117 Cerne Abbas & Bere Regis 1:25 000
OS Landranger Map 193 Taunton & Lyme Regis 1:50 000
OS Landranger Map 194 Dorchester & Weymouth 1:50 000

*Terrain*
Steep rolling countryside linked by deep valleys with long technical
climbs and descents.

*Facilities*
Beaminster is a small thriving town with plenty of pubs and cafes
for those pre and post ride moments. The public toilets are near the
entrance to the car park.
Revolutions 01308 420586
Bridport TIC 01308 424901 www.westdorset.com

*Introduction*
Please see the Beaminster West route for today's dilemma.

> *Links: East meets west. Plus the Hooke Park route at North
> Porton.*

*The Route*
1.  (ST482014) car park. From car park T-R, past the school,
    keep R at the Y-Junction following road as it turns to
    unclassified road and steep loose climb to road. T-R onto
    road for 600m to staggered bridleway junction; T-R onto

second bridleway following high ground along edge of field. Continue heading southeast along the high ground for 2.5km to second road junction.

2.  (ST509013) road junction. T-L onto road for 600m and T-L along minor road for 2km. Near bottom of long descent T-R onto bridleway adjacent Colt Wood Coppice and follow grassy trail heading southwest through field to track and climb past Coltleigh Farm to bridleway junction. T-L down steep loose rocky track to gate. Go through gate and continue down to bridleway junction in valley floor.

3.  (SY513993) bridleway junction. T-L towards wood and follow track up to R and onto flat ground; heading south along faint grassy trail and descend to L down short rocky track to road. T-L onto narrow road up towards North Porton. Just before N Porton T-R at Manor Farm and join unclassified road. Follow track for 2km down steep technical descent to narrow lane at Loscombe.

4.  (SY503979) Loscombe. 100m after joining lane T-R onto bridleway to Loscombe Farm then dog leg down through farmyard and continue to wood line. Take L-hand gate through wood; across stream to bridleway junction and T-L. Follow Jubilee Way up valley trail towards Mapperton House to second gate and estate road. After 300m T-L onto singletrack trail to field. T-R and follow to gate opposite and on to road.

5.  (SY496996) road junction. T-L onto road for 200m and T-R onto track and follow Jubilee Way for 1.6km to bridleway junction at edge of small wood; keep R (S-O) down excellent sunken singletrack trail to main road and T-R back into Beaminster.

*Route 30 Beaminster East:*
*The best climbs are also the best downhills.*

# 31. Hell Lane

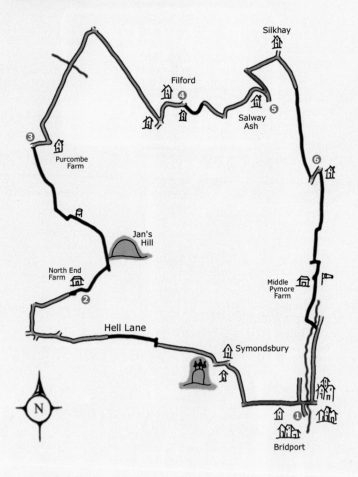

**West Dorset**

## 31.   Hell Lane
Moderate - 26km (16miles)
2-3 hours

Start/Finish: Long stay car park (SY463929) next to the bus station in Bridport.

*Maps*
OS Explorer Map 116 Lyme Regis & Bridport 1:25 000
OS Landranger Map 193 Taunton & Lyme Regis 1:50 000

*Terrain*
Rolling countryside with a clay base providing us with excellent technical climbs and descents especially when wet! Sweeping singletrack, grassy bridleways and country lanes (just to clear your tyres mind!).

*Facilities*
Bridport is a very busy and interesting market town and the Saturday street market is a must! There's plenty of choice on and off the high street for pubs and cafes, plus the Cafe Royal at the start is worth a mention; as are the public toilets!
Revolutions 01308 420586
Bridport TIC 01308 424901 www.westdorset.com

*Introduction:*
It's certainly more fun to ride down Hell Lane but still no walk in the park!
The route takes us inland giving a compact but otherwise challenging route over to Coppet Hill and the surrounding high ground and a real find in the unclassified road north of Purcombe Farm.

*Links: Do this route in reverse and link up with the Jurassic Coast ride the bottom of Hell Lane for an epic day out.*

### The route

1. (SY463929) Bus Station pay & display. Follow road out to roundabout and T-L. Carry S-O for 1.6km and T-R for Symondsbury. T-L alongside school in Symondsbury and T-R onto narrow lane and climb track to Quarry Cross track junction. Follow track to R then immediately L down Hell Lane and continue to road. Follow narrow road around north to Venn Farm and sharp R-hand bend to North End Farm.

2. (SY424949) North End Farm. Continue along track through farm to field and follow S-O up to gate on ridgeline. T-L and contour around L-hand side of Jan's Hill to gate. T-L through adjacent gate and follow hedgerow towards Coppet Hill for 1km to small water tank; T-L through gate and immediately T-R along hedge to gate. Follow slippery bridleway track down through fields to Farm access track.

3. (SY415964) access track. T-R to Purcombe Farm and T-L onto track between two fences; follow for 400m to two gates. Take R-hand gate and follow singletrack trail to narrow lane. Go S-O to main road. T-R onto main road for 2km and T-L onto farm access track opposite old press buildings for Filford. Continue to farmyard and T-R onto bridleway to narrow lane and bridleway junction.

4. (SY441975) lane/track junction. T-R onto bridleway and follow re-routed bridleway L beside large barns and T-R along track. End of track T-L into field and follow around into sunken boggy lane in gap in woodline; follow to Strongate Farm. Continue on narrow lane climbing to road junction at Salway Ash.

5. (SY455969) road junction. T-L onto road for 1.3km to minor road and T-R for Silkhay. At road junction above Silkhay T-R and head due south along unclassified road to T-junction. T-R along narrow lane for 1km to T-junction and T-L for 500m and T-R onto bridleway at Ash Lane

Farm. Follow track down through series of fields to gate at bottom; T-R through gate and re-join track to L and up to road junction.

6.  (SY463951) road junction. T-L for 150m and T-R towards Middle Pymore Farm. Follow track for 150m and T-L through bridleway gate and go S-A field (air strip?) to gate. Follow bridleway through two fields onto track to new housing complex and T-R at road junction with Pymore Road. Continue back into centre of Bridport to High St and T-R back to the start.

*Route 31 Hell Lane: There and back again!*

# 32. Jurassic Coast Ride

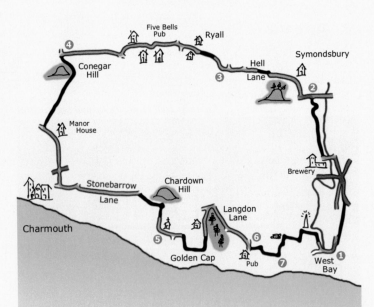

N

Five Bells
Pub

Ryall

Symondsbury

④

Conegar
Hill

Hell
Lane

③

②

Manor
House

Brewery

Stonebarrow
Lane

Chardown
Hill

Langdon
Lane

⑥

Charmouth

⑤

Golden Cap

Pub

⑦

West
Bay

①

## WEST DORSET

### 32. Jurassic Coast Ride
Moderate/Hard – 32km (20miles)
3-4 hours

Start/Finish: Pay & Display car park (SY466905) at West Bay one mile south of Bridport.
There maybe height restrictions at the entrance to the car park so watch out for any bikes on the roof of your vehicle!

*Maps*
OS Explorer Map 116 Lyme Regis & Bridport 1:25 000
OS Landranger Map 193 Taunton & Bridport 1 50 000

*Terrain*
Excellent all-weather surfaces along the coast and inland providing an interesting variety of trails.

*Facilities*
Plenty of pubs, cafes and fast food shacks in West Bay. Bridport is a thriving market town with a wonderful street market on Saturdays.
Revolutions Bridport 01308 420586
Bridport TIC: 01308 424901 www.westdorset.com
The Five Bells Pub in Whitchurch Canonicorum

*Introduction*
200 million years in the making. It's got to be good! The Jurassic Coastline in Dorset is a designated world heritage site and both the coastline and surrounding areas are truly stunning, as must be the marketing budget!

So, not withstanding millions of years to produce such to-pography and dinosaur prints, as a mountain biker, here is one of the few areas within the UK that you can legally ride near the coastline.

The route also takes us around and near the summit of Golden Cap; at 191m it's the highest point along the whole of the south coast.

*Links: Hell Lane or Eggardon Hill should satisfy the marathon rider.*

### The route

1. (SY466905) car park. Join national cycle route 2 at the rear of car park and T-L to road. T-L to roundabout and take third exit for town centre. At traffic lights beside Palmers brewery T-L. Go over bridge, T-R onto cycle path and follow river. At end of cycle path T-R over weak bridge and first L. Continue through car park to small roundabout on main road.

2. (SY464930) roundabout. T-L following main road west out of Bridport for 1.4km to minor road junction and T-R for Symondsbury. Follow road to T-junction T-L past school and T-R onto narrow lane; road becomes track and climb to Quarry Cross track junction. Go S-O joining Hell Lane and to road junction. Follow S-O along road for 400m to sharp bend; go S-O and keep R to join unclassified road.

3. (SY418942) track/bridleway. Continue along track to large field and follow grassy trail up through to join track above Butt Farm. Carry S-O into Ryall to road junction and go S-O down past pub and into Whitchurch Canonicorum. At crossroads at end of village, T-R and follow Becklands Lane for 1.5km to summit of hill.

4. (SY366945) T-L opposite road junction onto narrow bridleway and climb through field to gate at edge of wood. Follow bridleway track along high ridgeline through series of fields and gates southwest to road. Track/road junction.
   T-L onto road and follow over A35 to T- junction. T-L for 300m and T-R climbing Stonebarrow Lane. Continue through long car park area to two gates; take R-hand gate following grassy trail down to join stony track and follow to L. Contour around below Chardown Hill to track junction in Upcot and

T-L. Follow track for 400m and T-R down to St Gabriel's Church.

5. (SY402924) St Gabriel's Church. Follow the bridleway up past the remains of St Gabriel's and past first hedge line to second hedge and T-R up towards Golden Cap. Follow track around L to gate and drop down diagonally L to second gate and into following field towards Filcombe Farm. Drop down L to gate and into farm yard; continue to road and T-R. At top of climb T-R onto narrow lane, past a mast and T-L onto track (Langdon Lane) for 1.6km to road.

6. (SY420922) road junction. T-R into Seatown. (it's worth visiting the Anchor pub here). T-L at caravan park entrance onto concrete bridleway track for 250m and T-L through wooden gate to second gate and T-L following faint grassy trail contouring up around rear of Red Cliff. Climb up steeply to thin treeline and T-L onto track and to gate. T-L through gate and follow fence line around to L around rear of Dog House Hill and climb steep track to path/bridleway junction.

7. (SY434915) path/bridleway junction. T-L to gate and follow narrow trail down between Thorncombe Beacon and small Knoll for 400m and T-L (teas at Down House Farm) to Down House Farm. T-R past farm into field and continue down to Lower Eype and another pub! T-L uphill for 400m and T-R onto bridleway track. Go S-A road towards mast and down to gate. T-R through narrow gate onto singletrack trail; follow to road. Carry S-O and T-R down into West Bay and follow road to car park.

*Route 32 Jurrassic Coast Ride:*
*200 million years in the making, the trails have got to be good!*

*Classic Jurrasic Singletrack.*

# 33. Tour of Wooton Hill

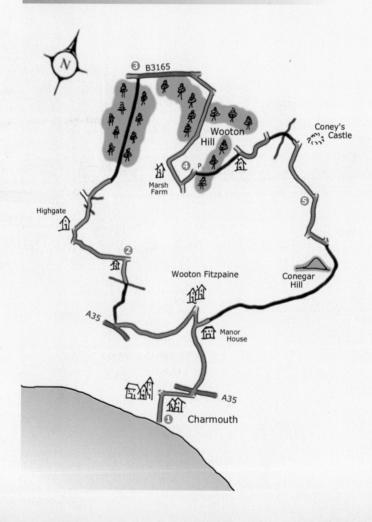

## WEST DORSET

## 33.  Tour of Wooton Hill
Hard – 25km (15.5miles)
3-4 hours

Start/Finish: Car park on the sea front at Charmouth (SY365931) 3km East of Lyme Regis.

*Maps*
OS Explore Map 116 Lyme Regis & Bridport 1:25 000
OS Landranger Map 193 Taunton & Lyme Regis 1:50 000

*Terrain*
Steep hills and valleys; offering up difficult technical riding at a very a slow pace but well linked by excellent all weather tracks and farm access roads.

*Facilities*
Charmouth offers plenty of seaside shops pubs, cafes and has more campsites than anywhere else in Dorset. Please note that there are no facilities here other than at Charmouth.
Revolutions 01308 420586
Lyme Regis TIC 01297 442138 www.westdorset.com

*Introduction*
If I had put this route at the beginning of the book I don't think many readers would have turned to the next page. This mini adventure is hard going, so let's start at sea level for a guaranteed downhill finish.

*Links: The Jurassic coast ride; if you're up for it!*
***The route***
1.  (SY365931) car park. Return to the high street and T-R for 400m before T-L up over the A35 and follow to Y-junction

next to village hall in Wootton Fitzpaine. T-L and climb narrow lane for 2km and T-R through small gap in hedgerow, just before reaching the A35. Follow technical bridleway track down to small ford and continue up unclassified road to crossroads.

2.  (SY353960) crossroads. T-L past Bowshot Farm for 2km to crossroads and T-R towards Highgate. At bottom of steep descent (300m) T-R onto track and follow down into hollow at bridleway junction; start climbing and T-R at next track junction. Continue over stream to gate and contour up and around L through field (above pond) to gate in wood line ahead. Follow into wood and go S-O at main track for1.4km to main road.

3.  (SY351986) road junction. T-R onto road for 1km and T-R onto Fish Pond Bottom Road for 350m and T-R again onto bridleway track heading southwest for 1km to road junction and go S-O for 400m and S-O again to bridleway towards Marsh Farm. Follow bridleway for 1km to road and T-L. Continue uphill for 600m and T-R into small car park at Wooton Hill.

4.  (SY353969) car park. Follow trail S-O up between staggered fallen trees (not all weather track to right) through woods heading northeast down to bridleway junction with open field. Head across field to gate. T-R onto road for 500m to sharp corner at Sheepwash Farm; follow singletrack down over stream and up to trail junction at Little Coombe Farm. T-R onto farm access track and follow to road junction

5.  (SY373969) road junction. T-R onto road for 1.2km to road junction and T-L uphill for 400m and T-R opposite road junction onto narrow bridleway. Follow to woods at Conegar Hill and continue along high ridgeline for 3km to road above Catherston Leweston. T-L and follow road back over A35 to T-junction; turning R back into Charmouth and the start.

*Route 33 Tour of Wooton Hill:*
*Making the most of the open going.*

Breaking loose

*'The mass of men lead lives of quiet desperation', and few realise their dreams of escape. Dave Cook followed his dream and in 1989 set off for Australia on his bicycle. His vivid account tells of his rock-climbing adventures en route, of friends made and of the political situations he found including a tangle with Saddam Hussein's police.*

*Throughout he records with keen observation and refreshing honesty his reflections on social injustice from Yugoslavia to the Indian continent; and on his own moral values and the pursuit of dreams.*

# The Ernest Press Mountain Bike Guide series

Inverness, the Great Glen & the Cairngorms: **£8.50**

The Highlands
**£15.00**

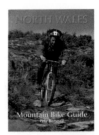

North Wales: **£8.25**

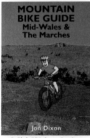

Mid-Wales & the Marshes: **£7.50**

Kent: **£6.95**

Wiltshire: **£8.50**

County Durham:
**£7.50**

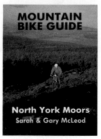

North York Moors:
**£7.50**

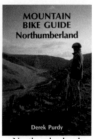

Northumberland:
**£12.00**

# Browse and buy online at www.ernest-press.co.uk

The Lake District, Howgills & Yorkshire Dales: **£9.00**

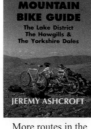

More routes in the Lakes, Howgills & ... **£8.50**

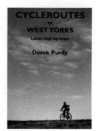

Cycleroutes in West Yorks – Lanes and by-ways: **£7.50**

West Yorkshire: **£8.50**

Mid Yorkshire, Rye Dale & the Wolds: **£7.50**

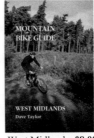

West Midlands: **£8.00**

East Midlands: **£7.95**

Derbyshire and the Peak District(1) **£8.50**

Derbyshire & the Peak District **£8.50**